Simone Sereni

Simphony of Colors

A Colorful Journey through Magic Musical Instruments

Coloring Book

ISBN: 9798857714065

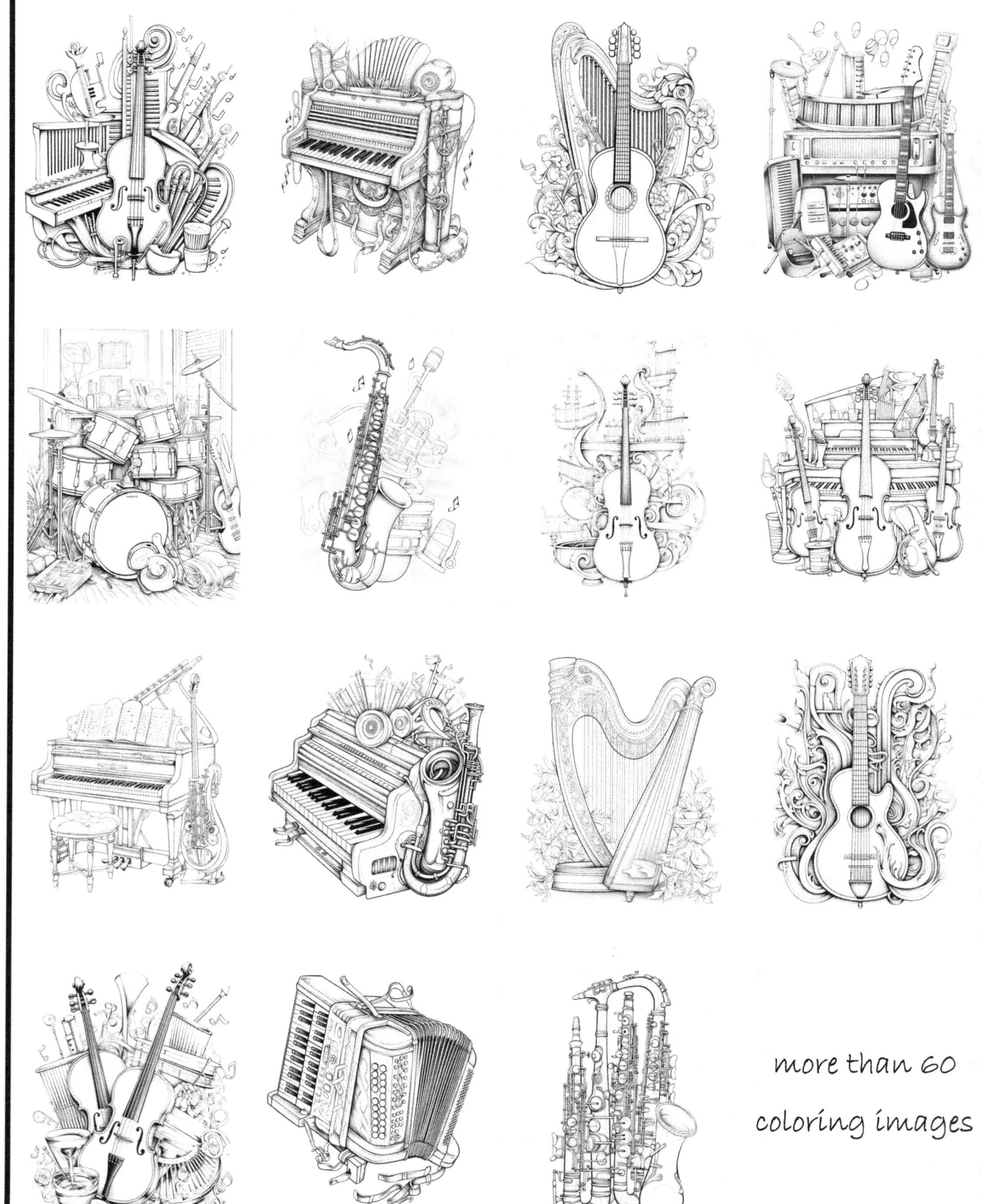

more than 60 coloring images

Color Test Page

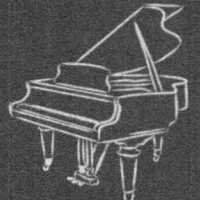

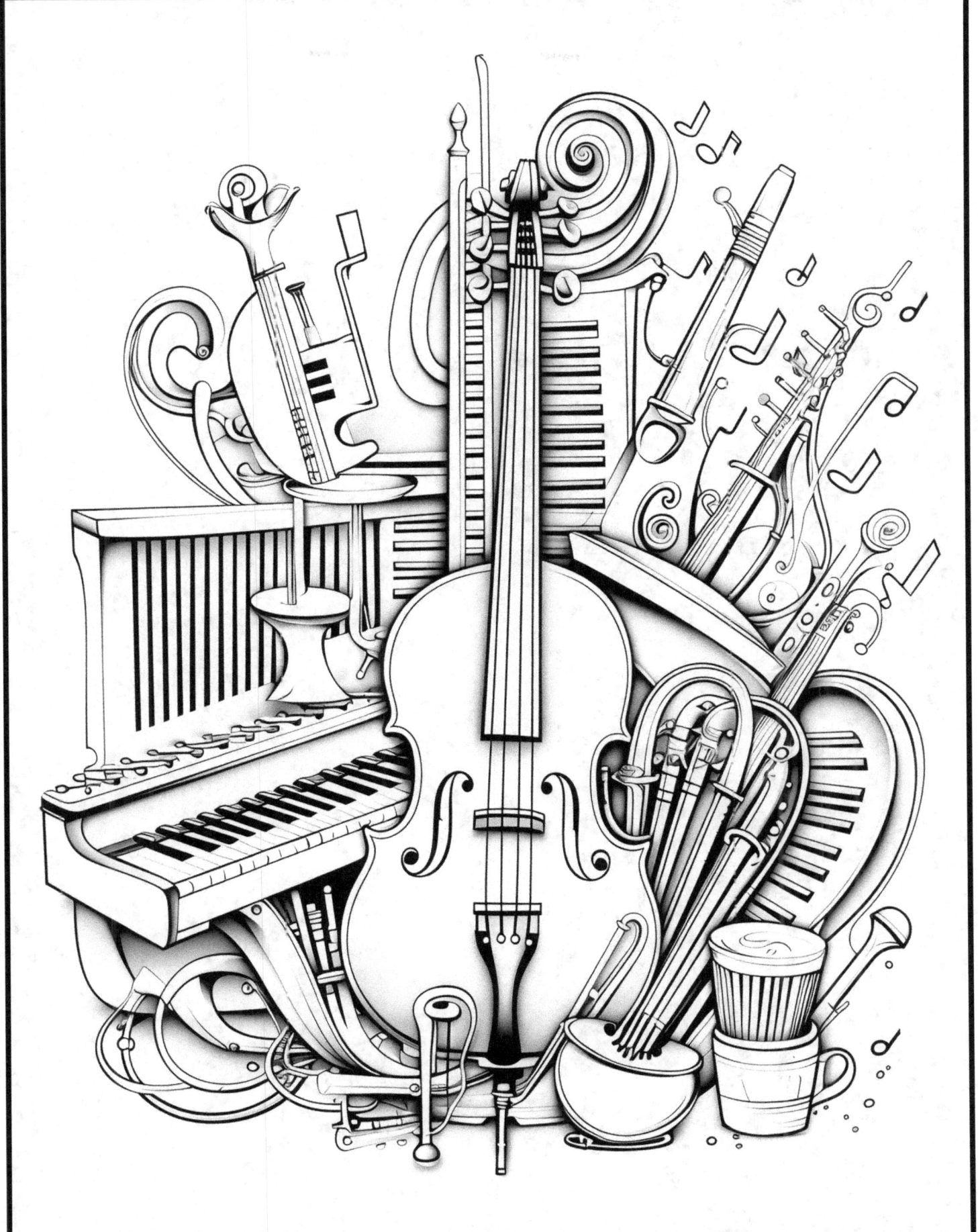

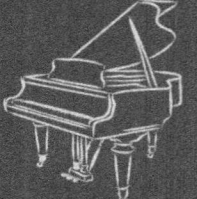

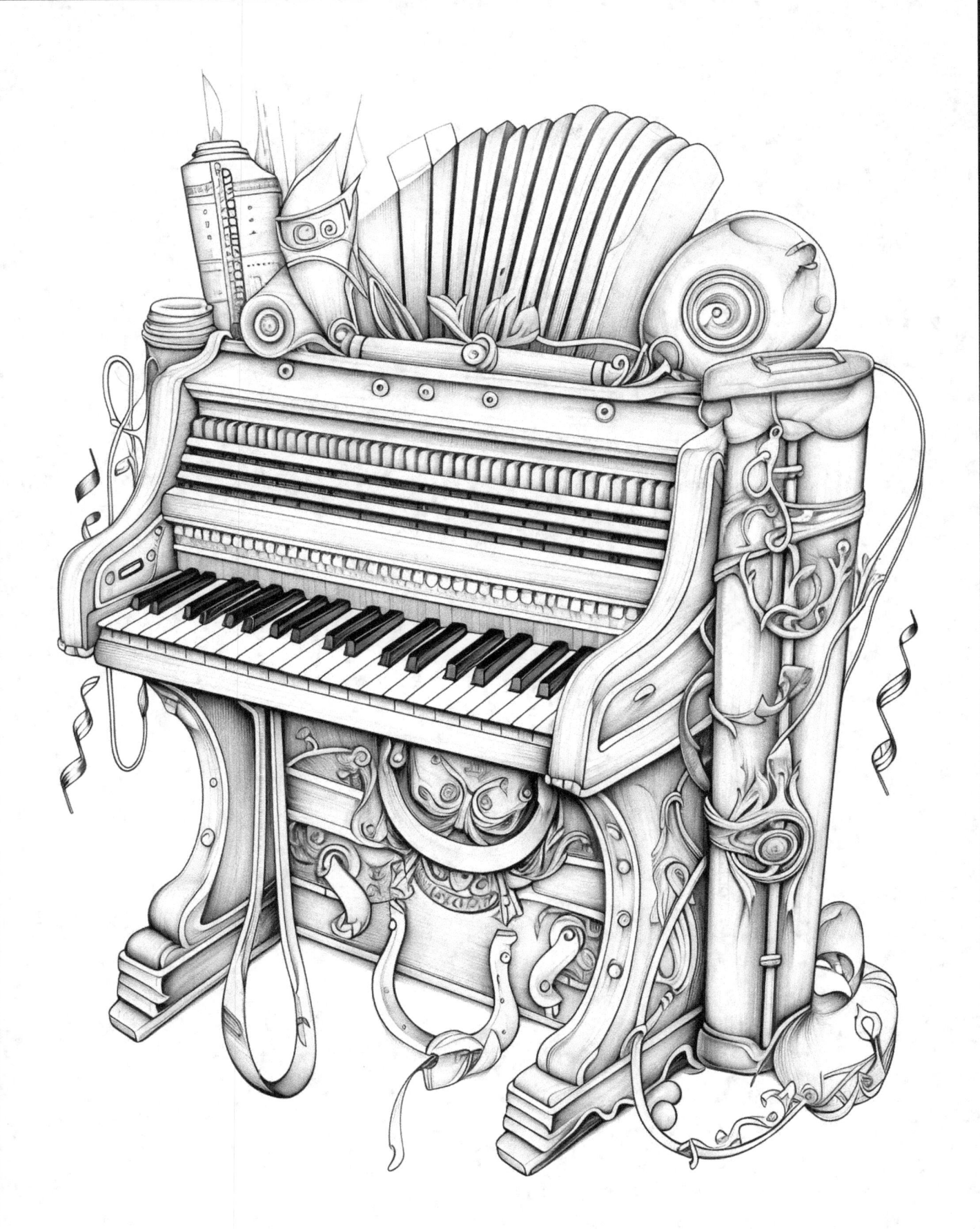

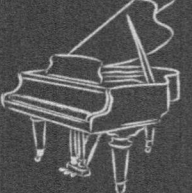

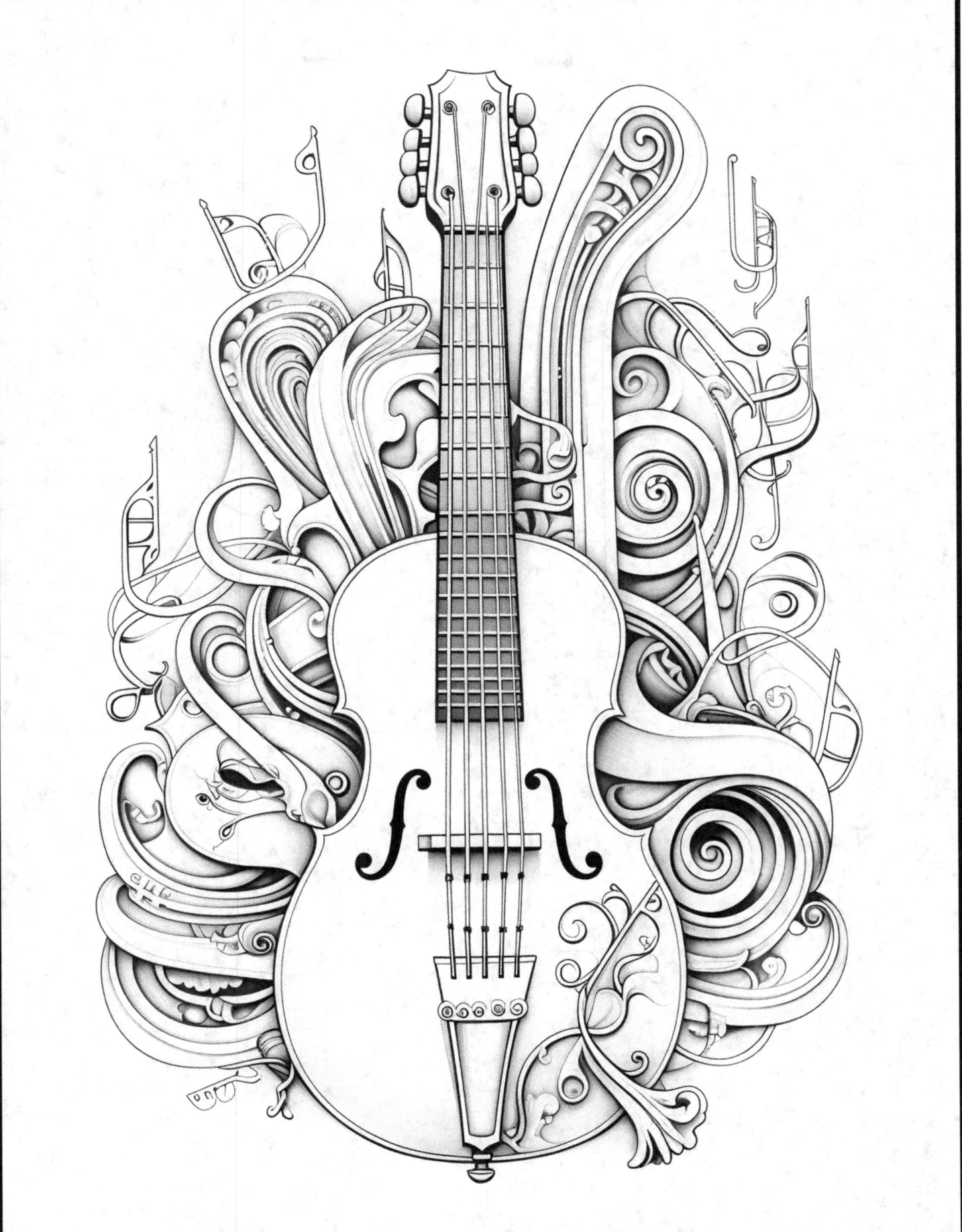

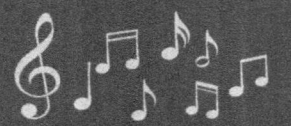
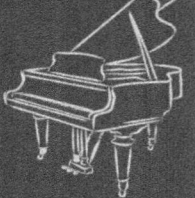

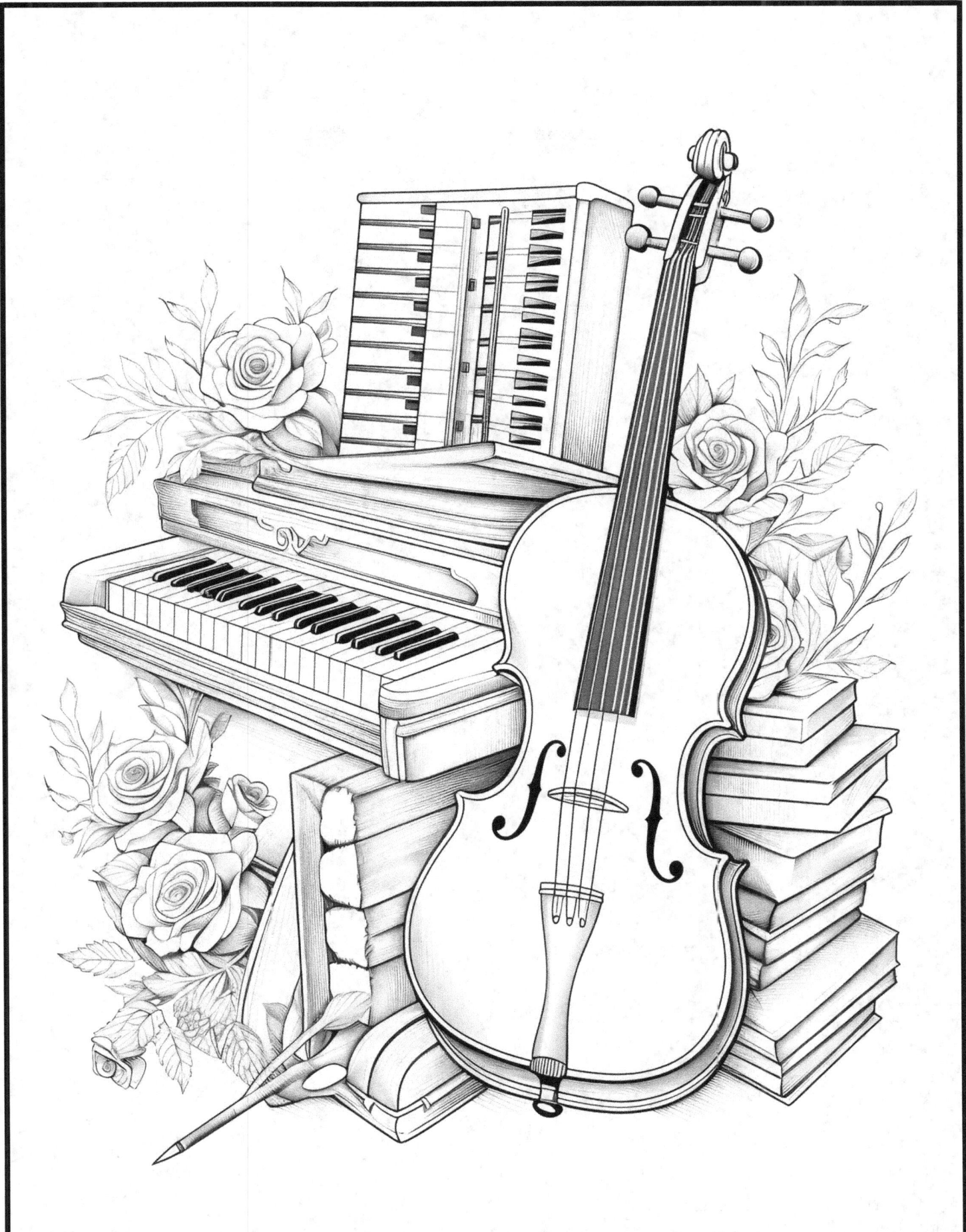

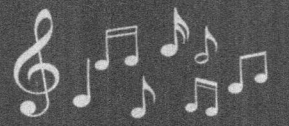
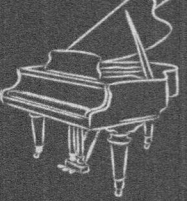

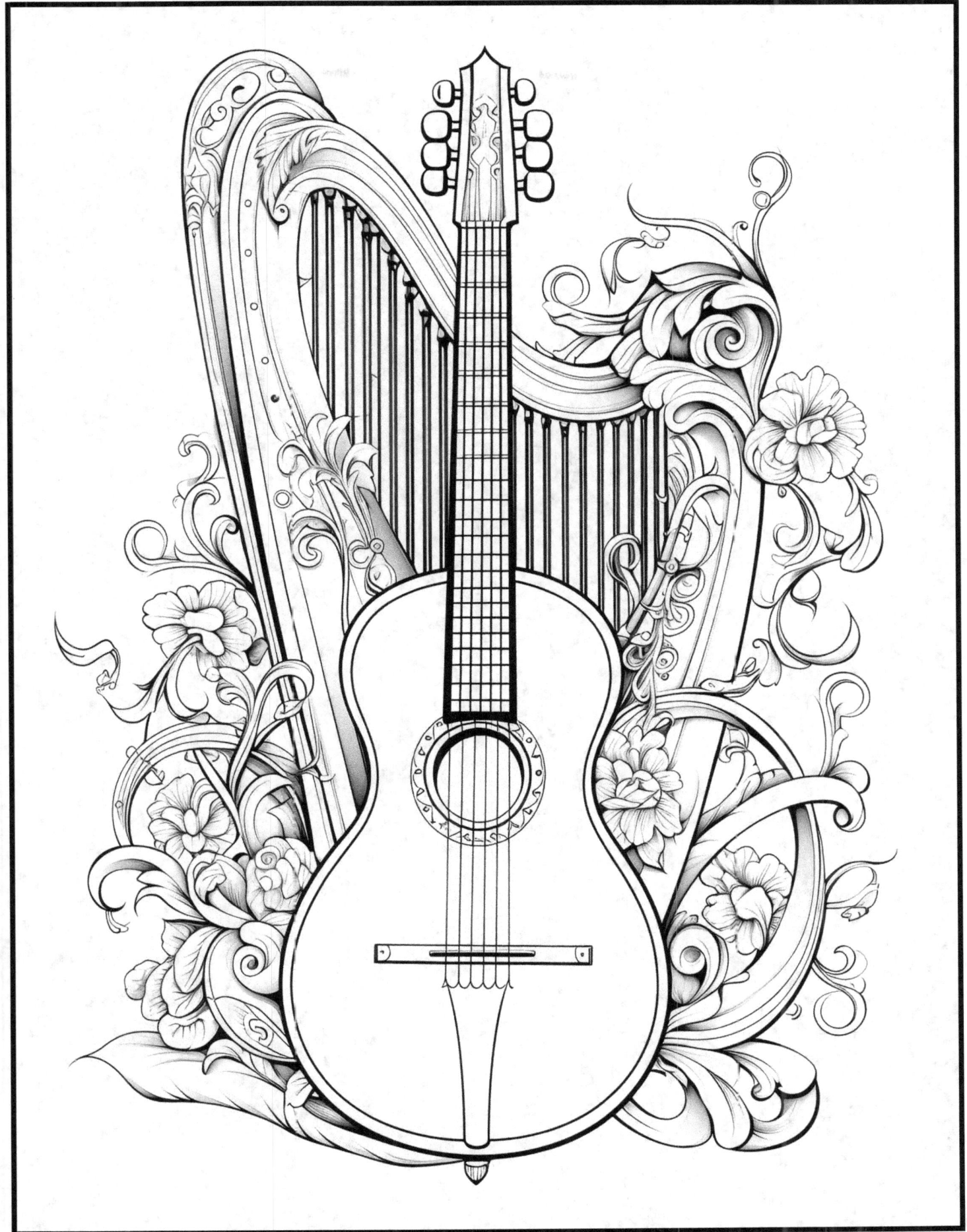

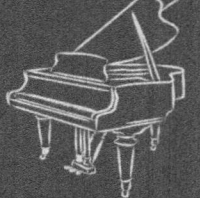

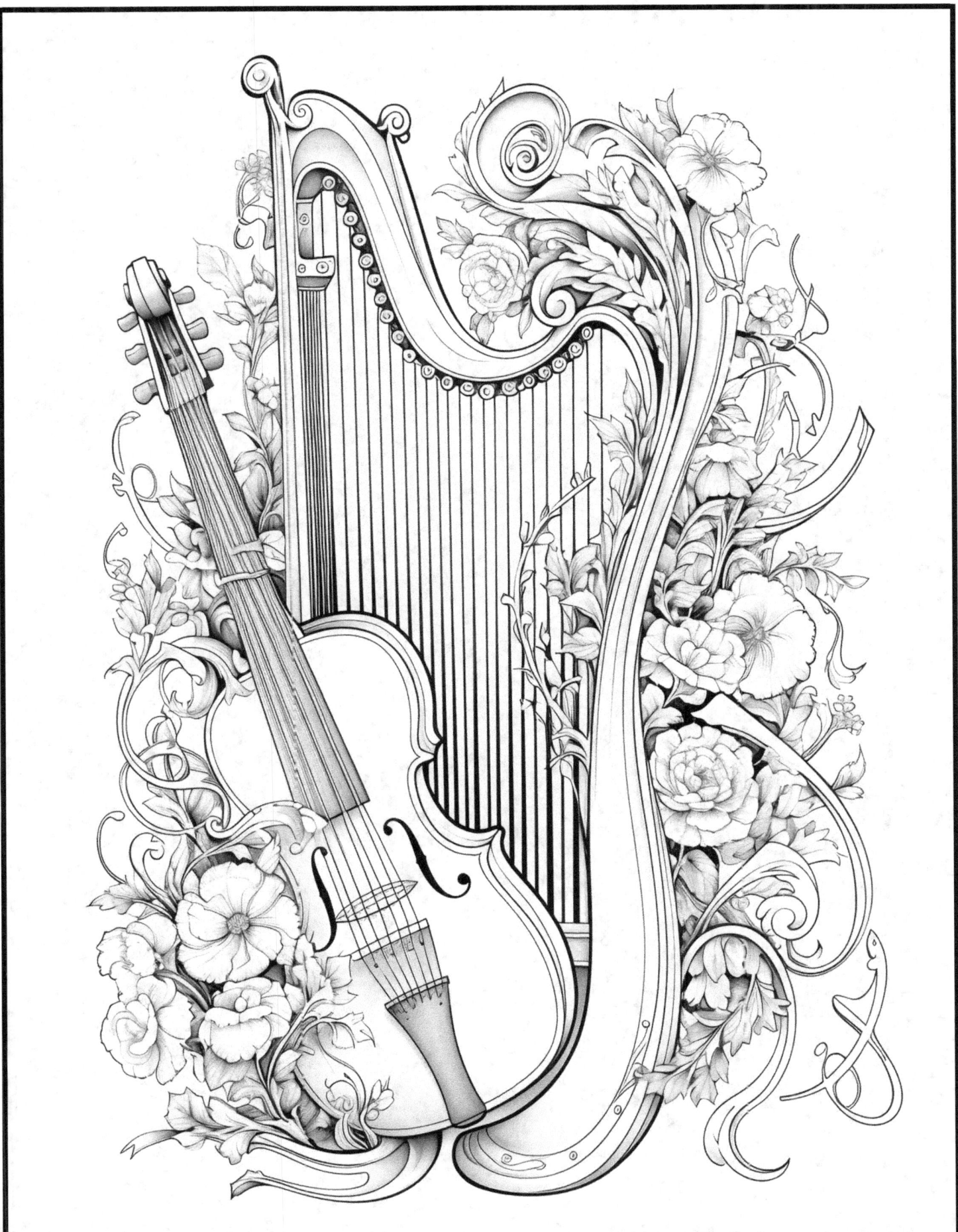

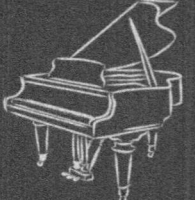

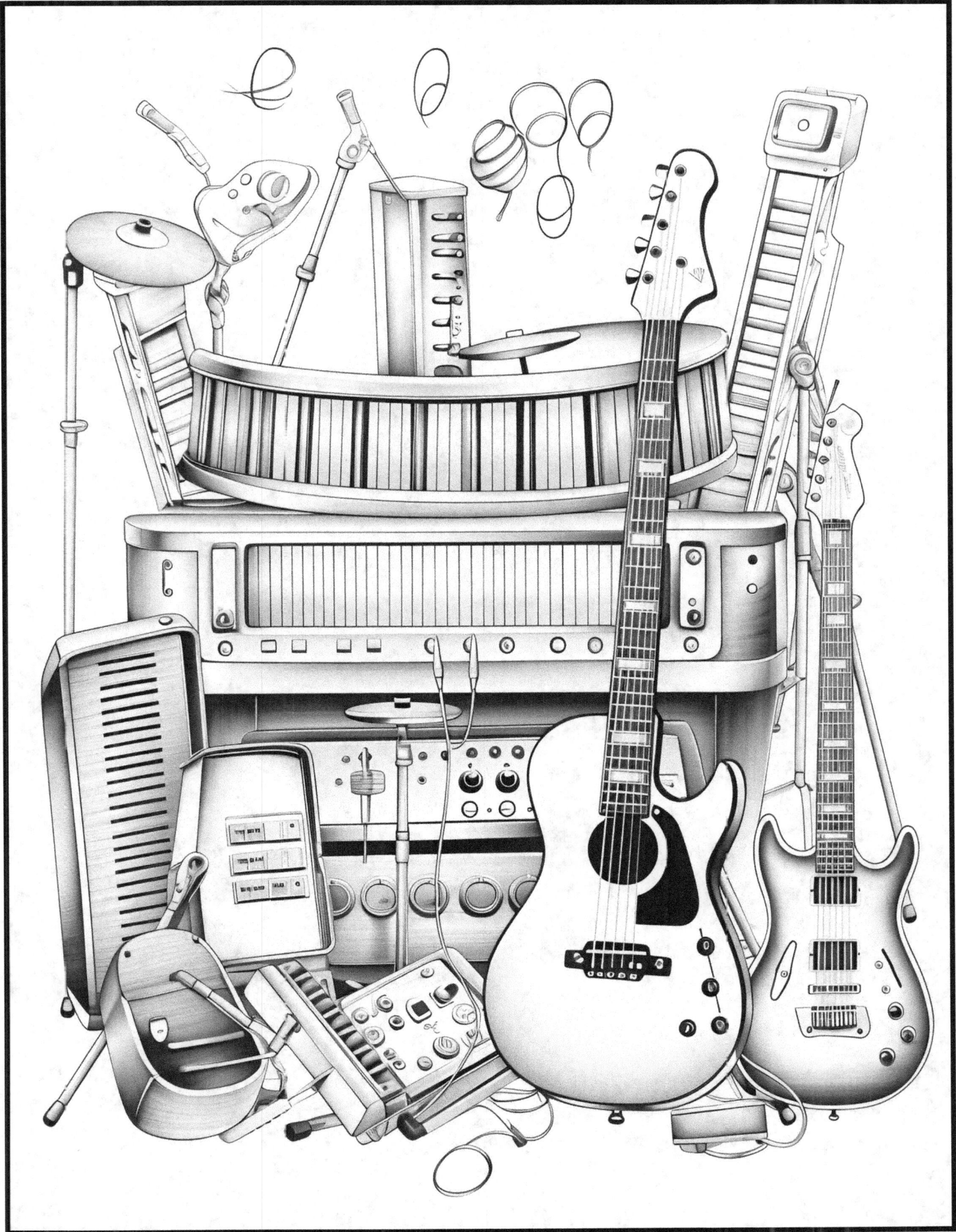

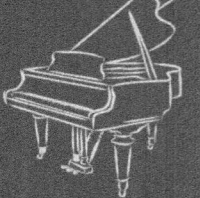

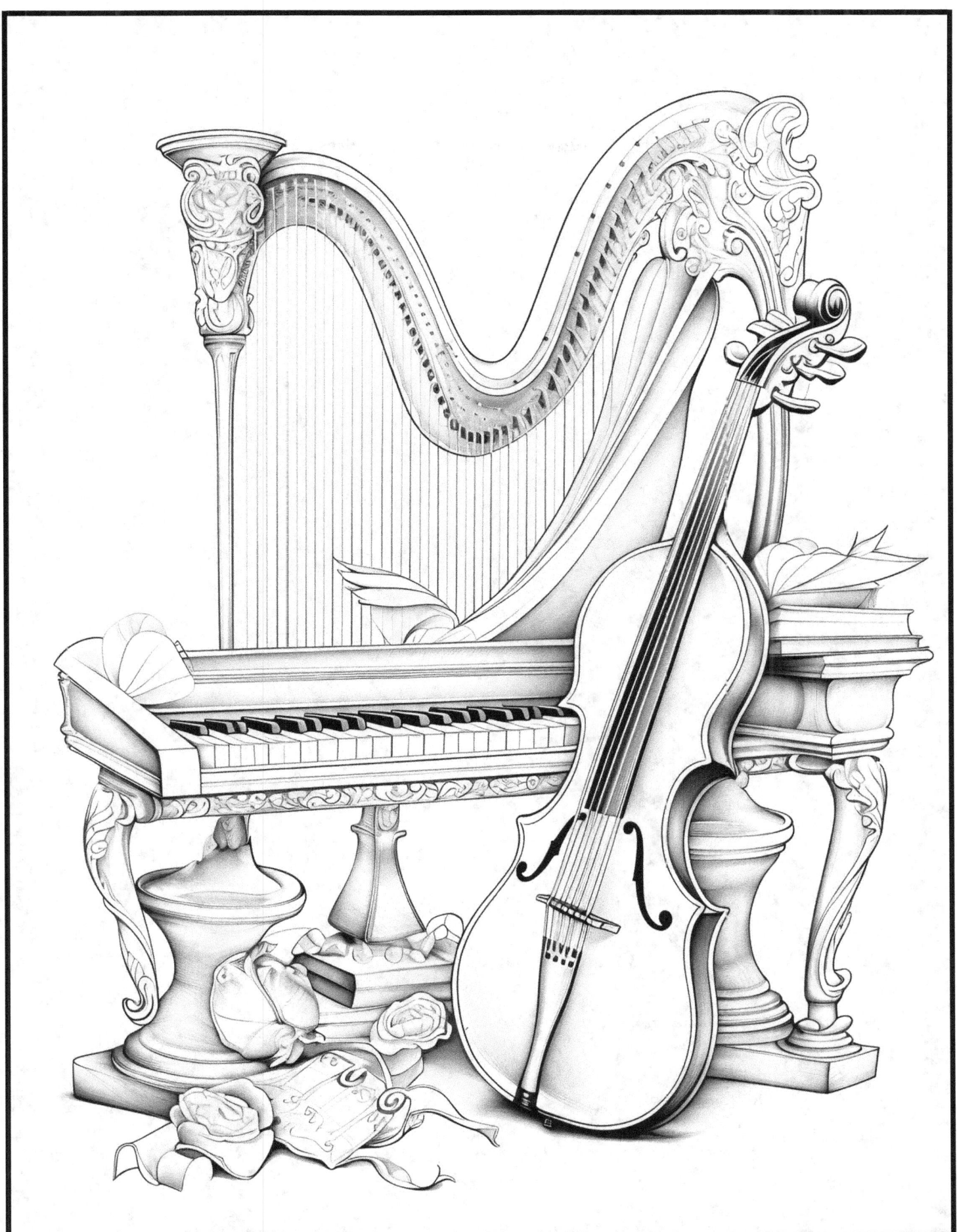

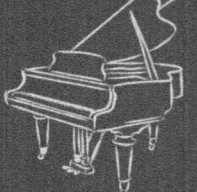

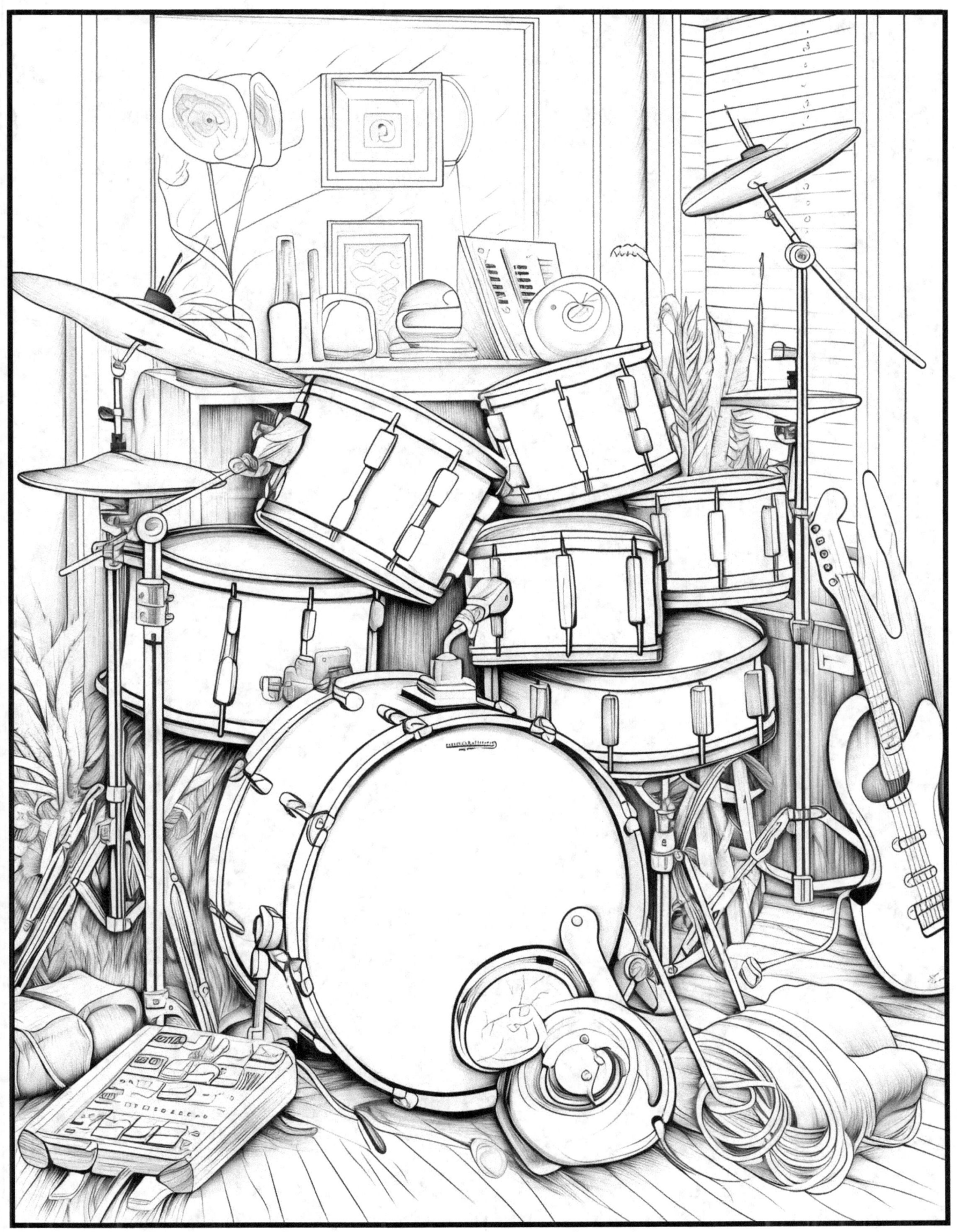

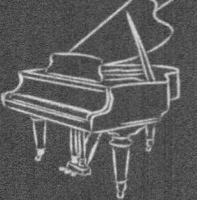

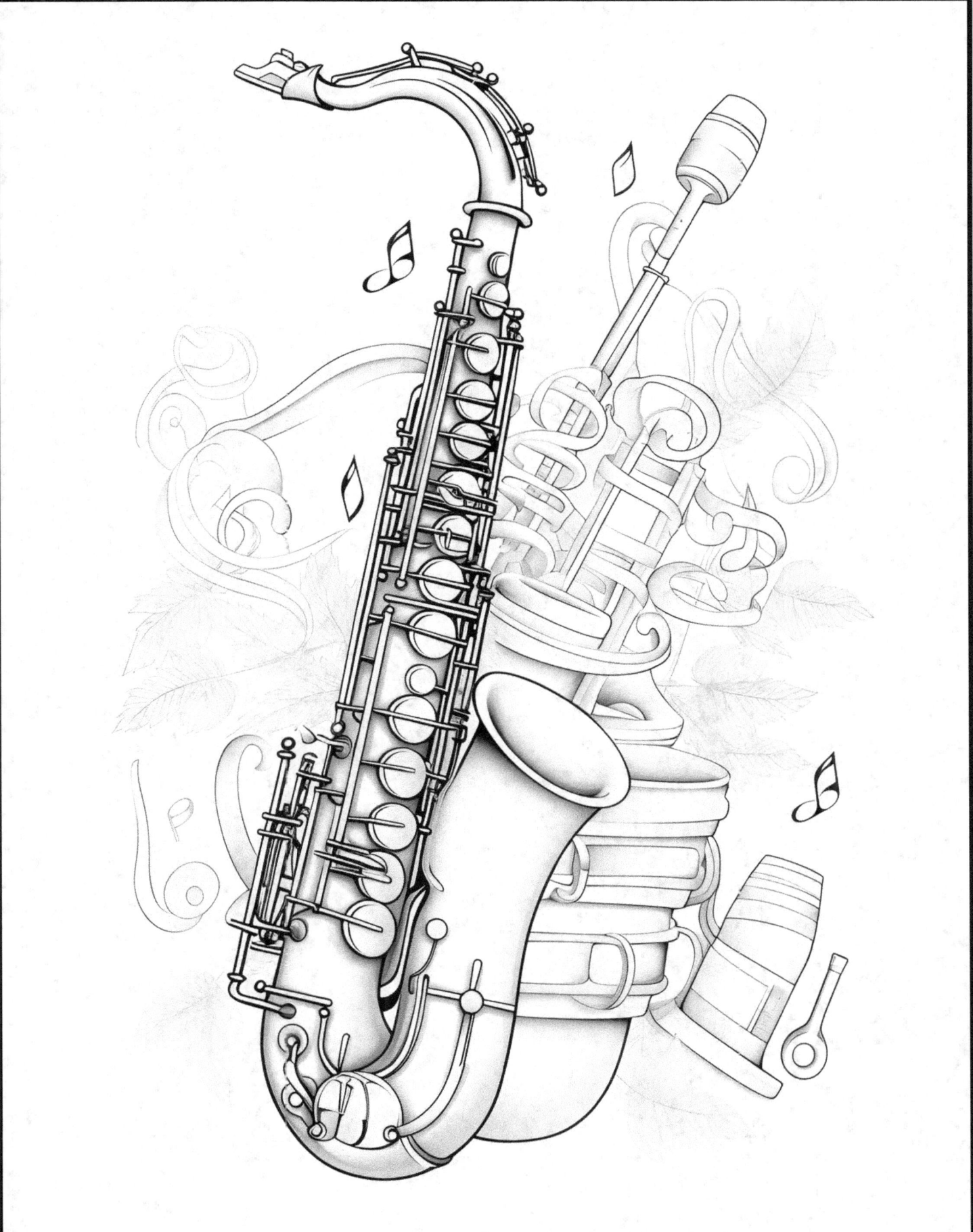

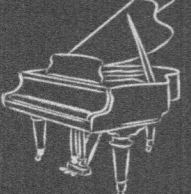

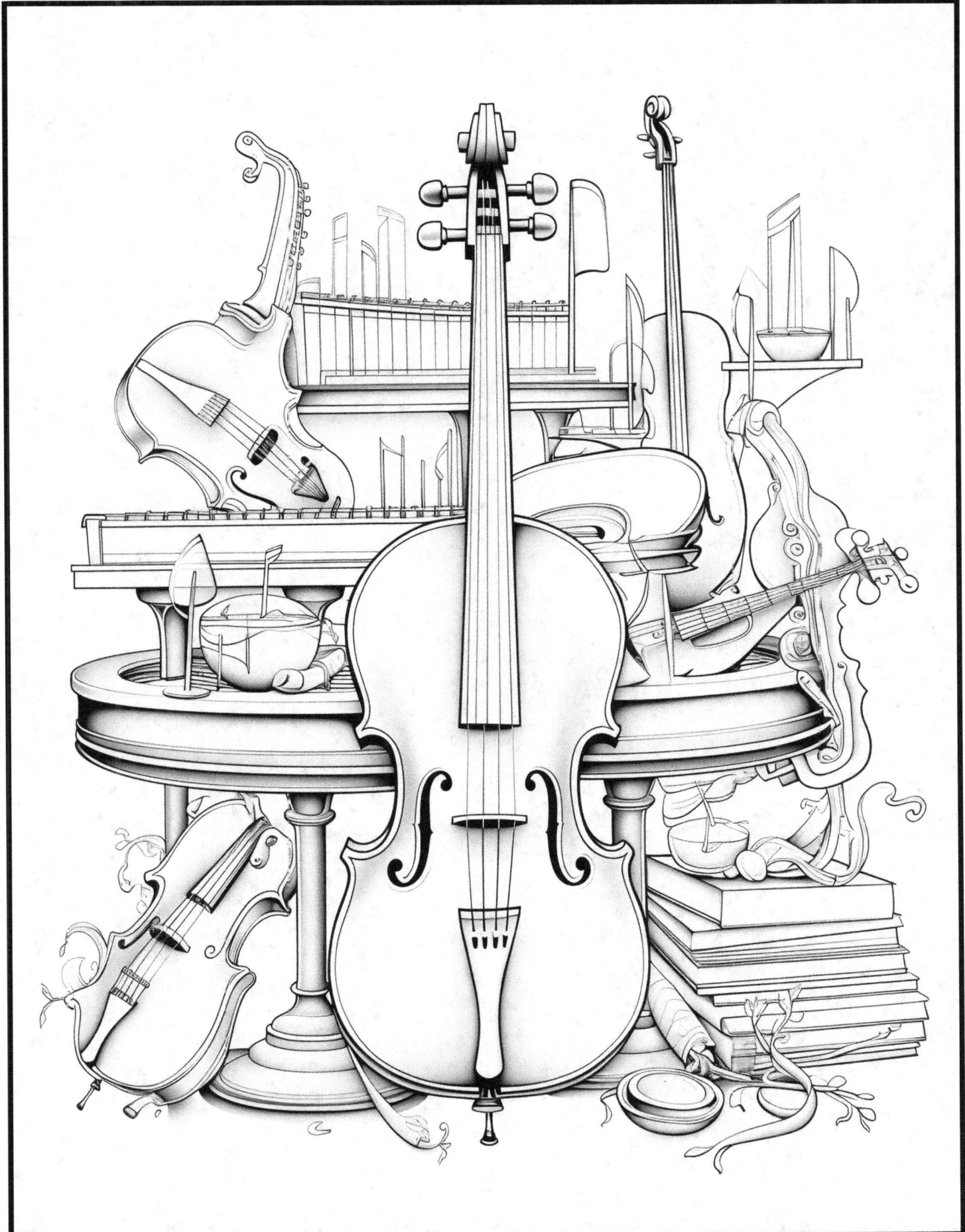

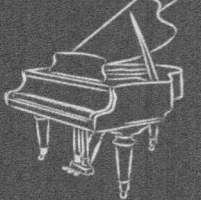

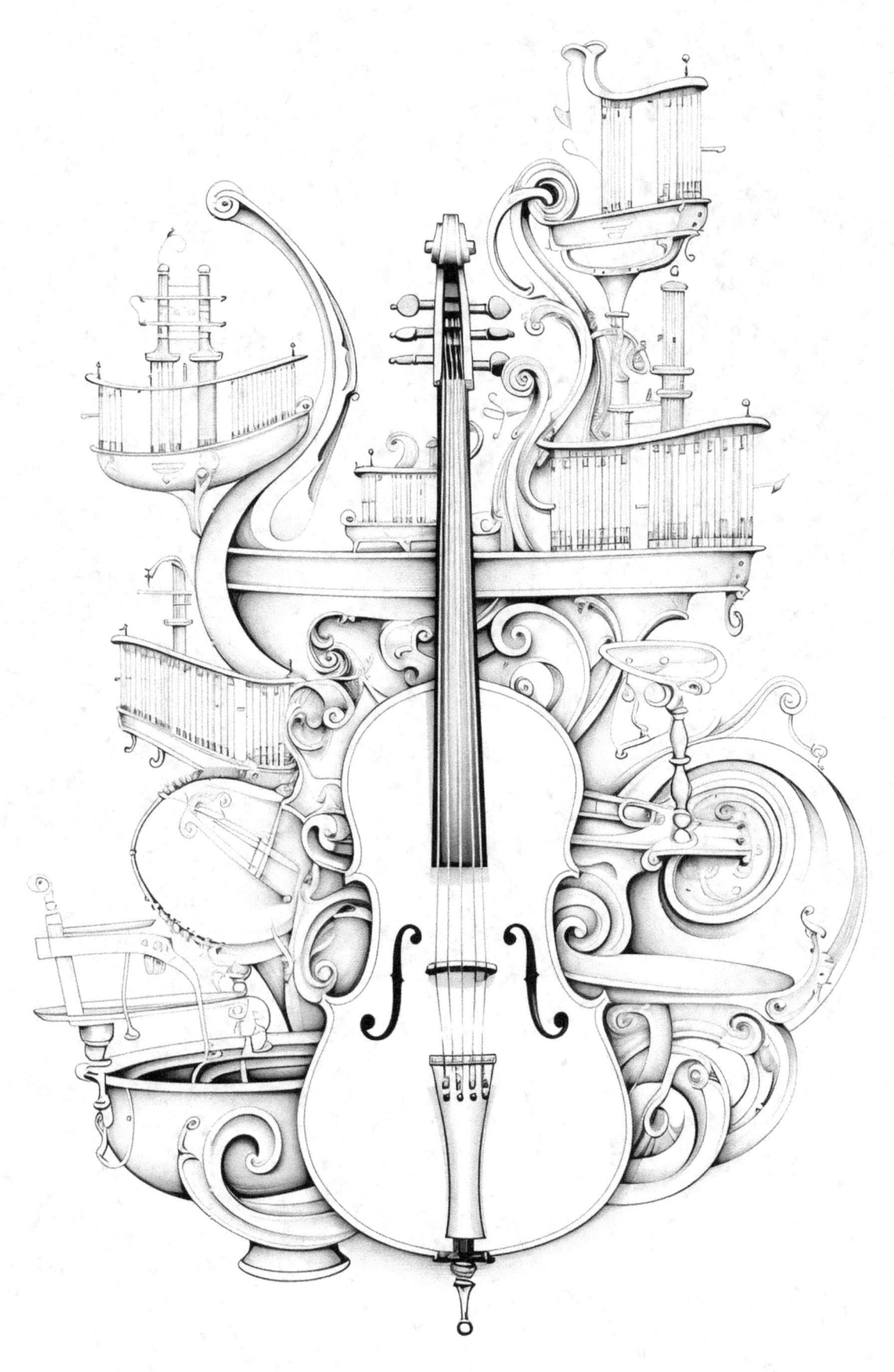

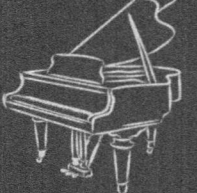

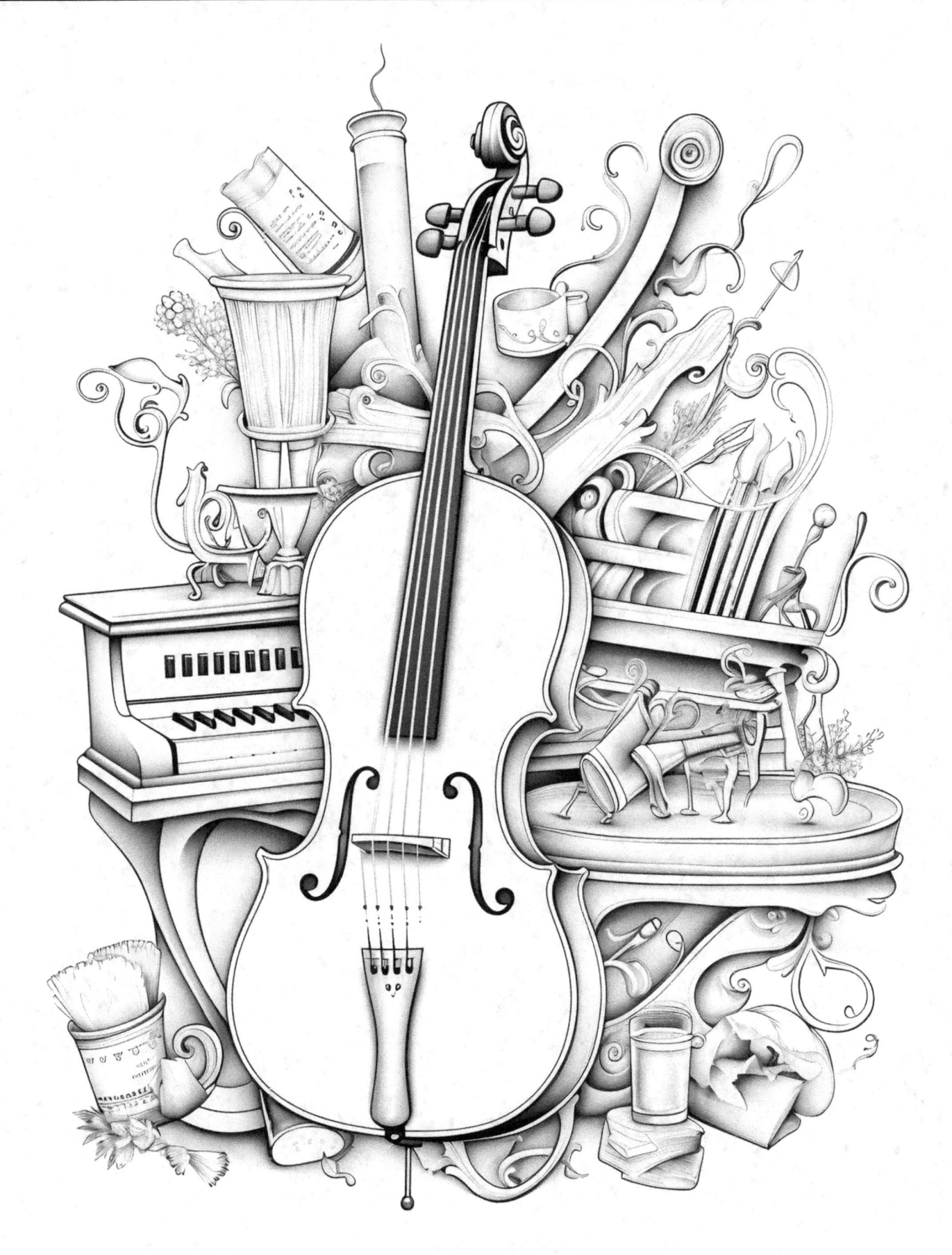

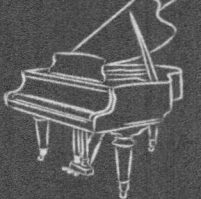

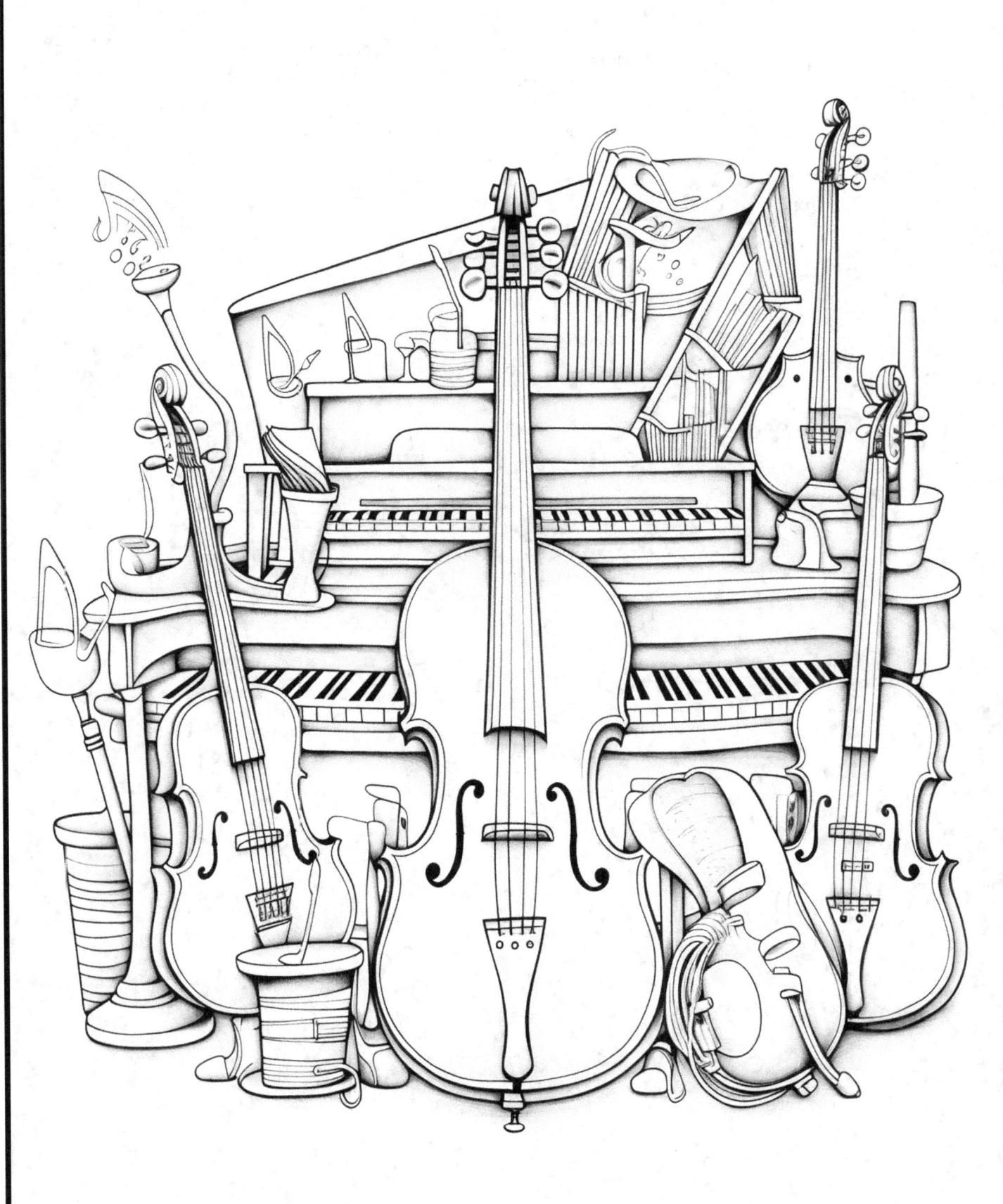

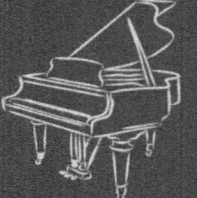

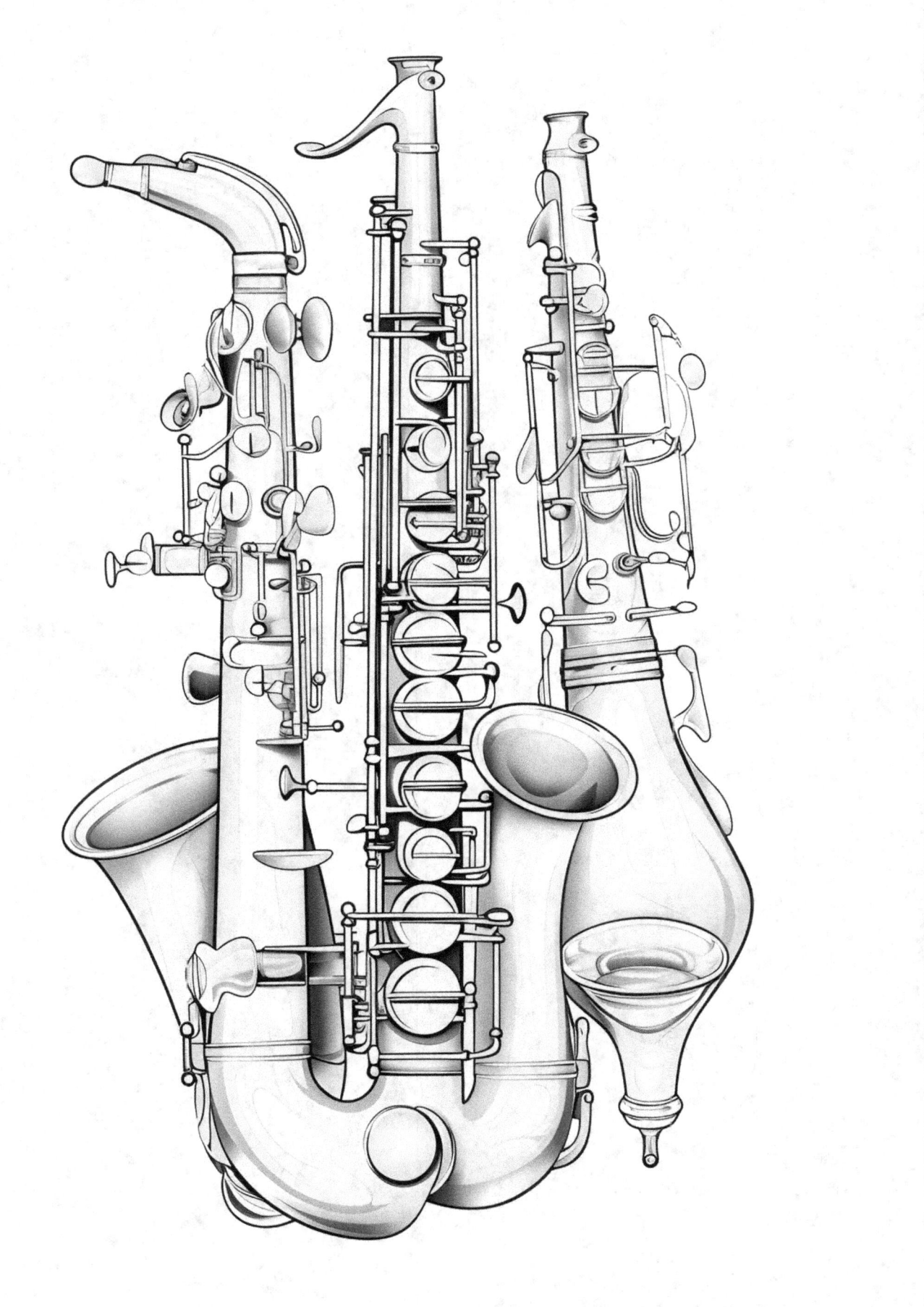

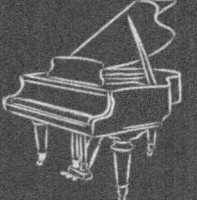

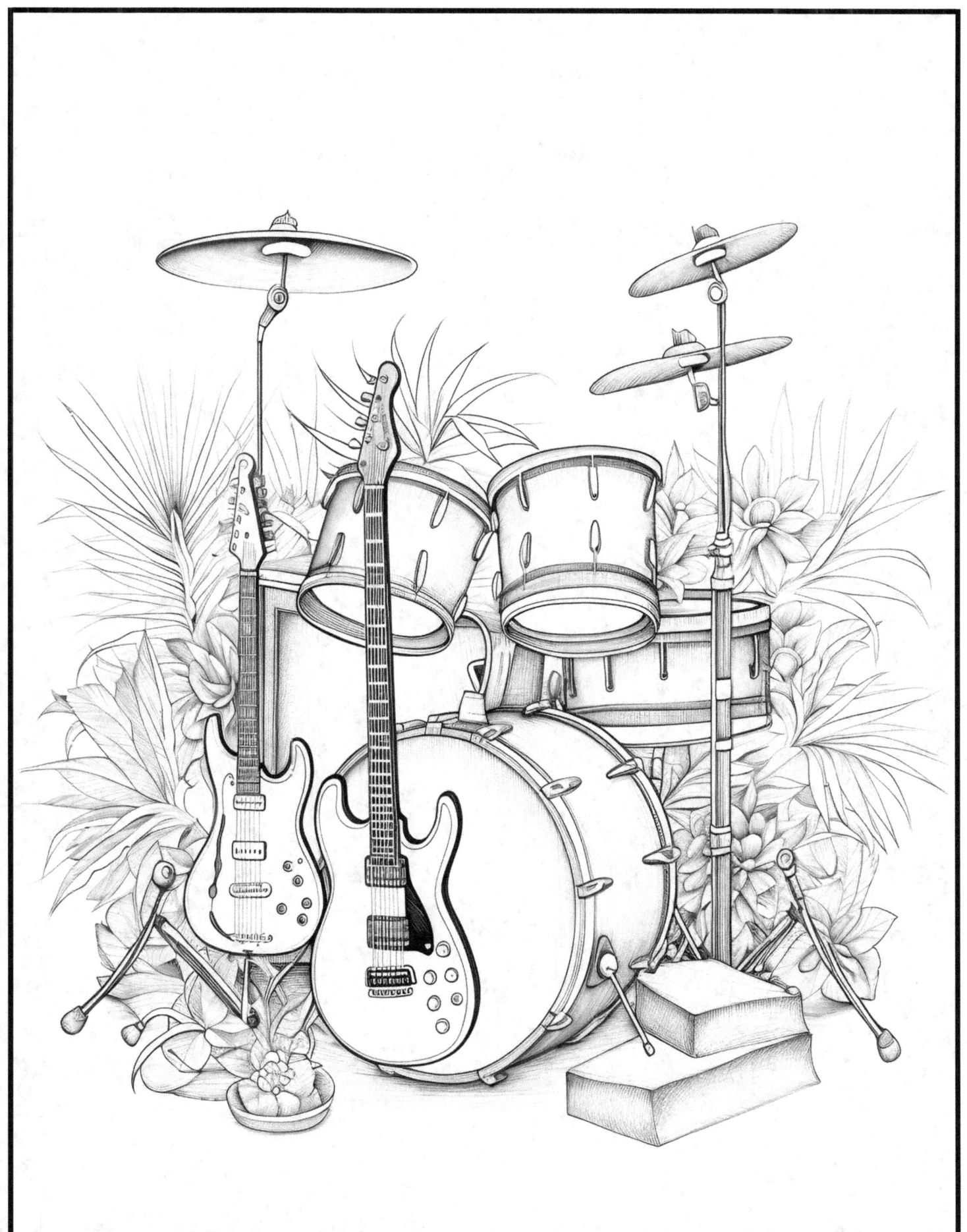

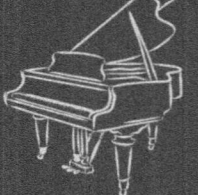

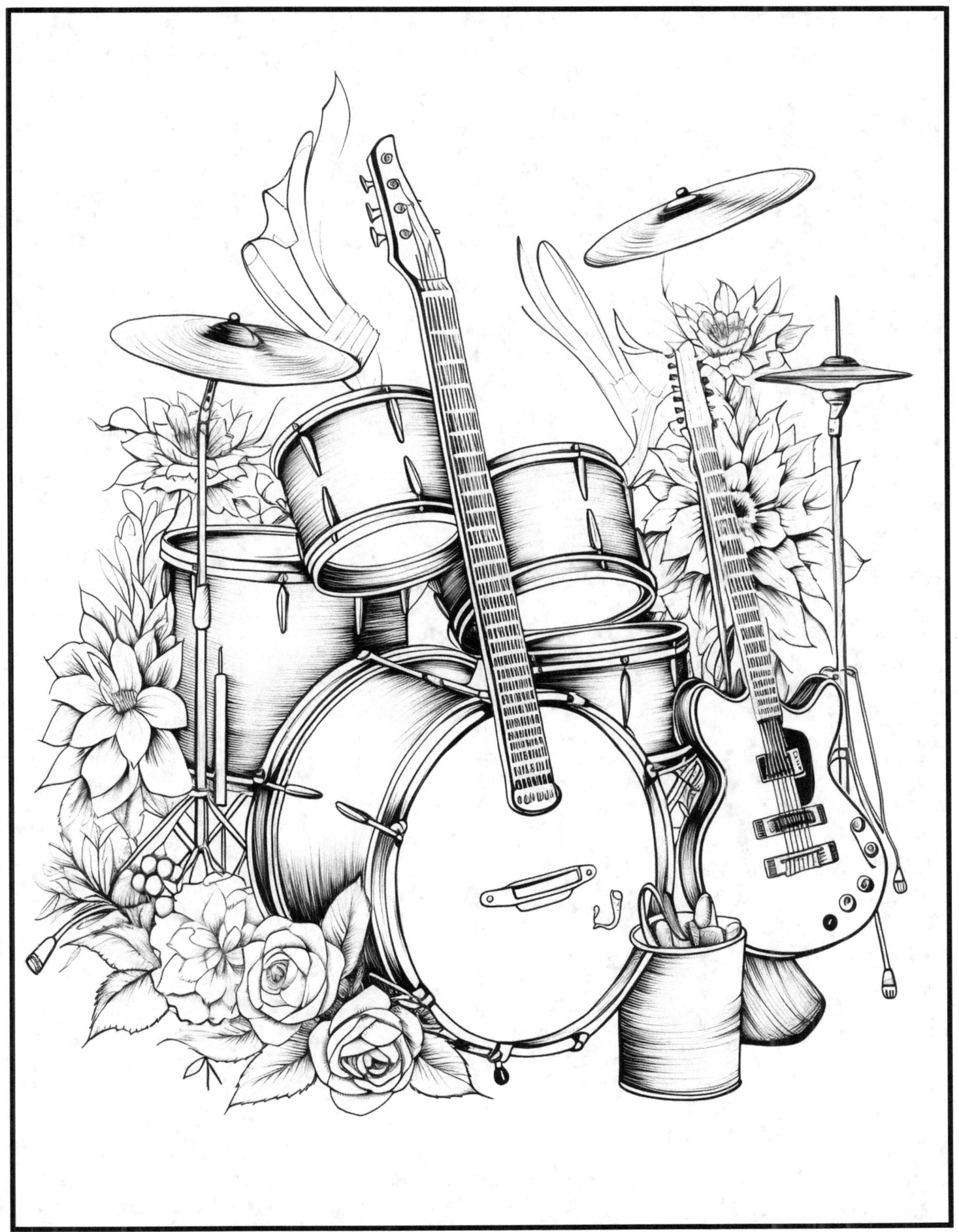

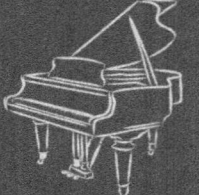

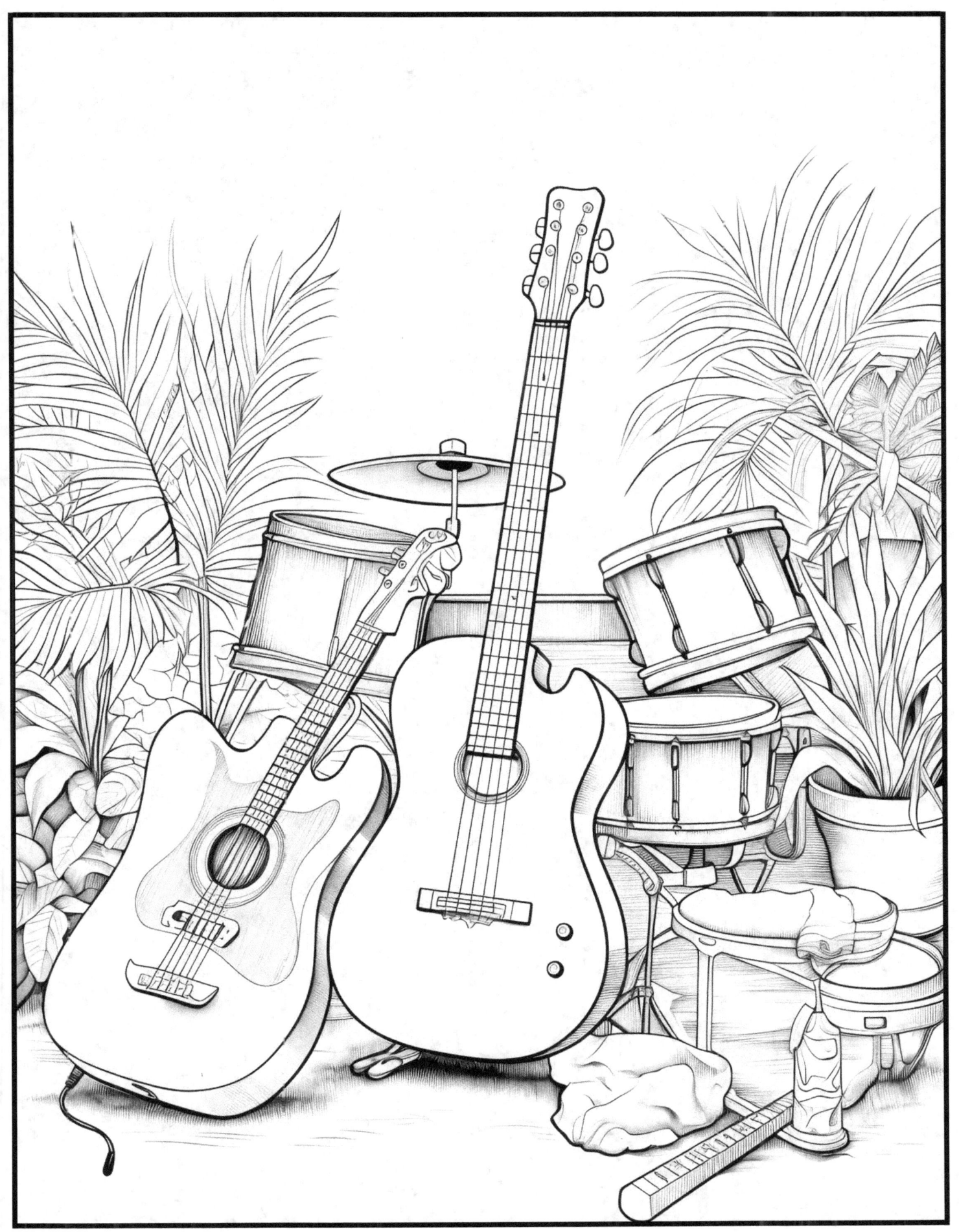

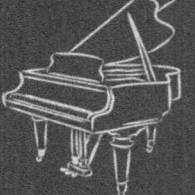

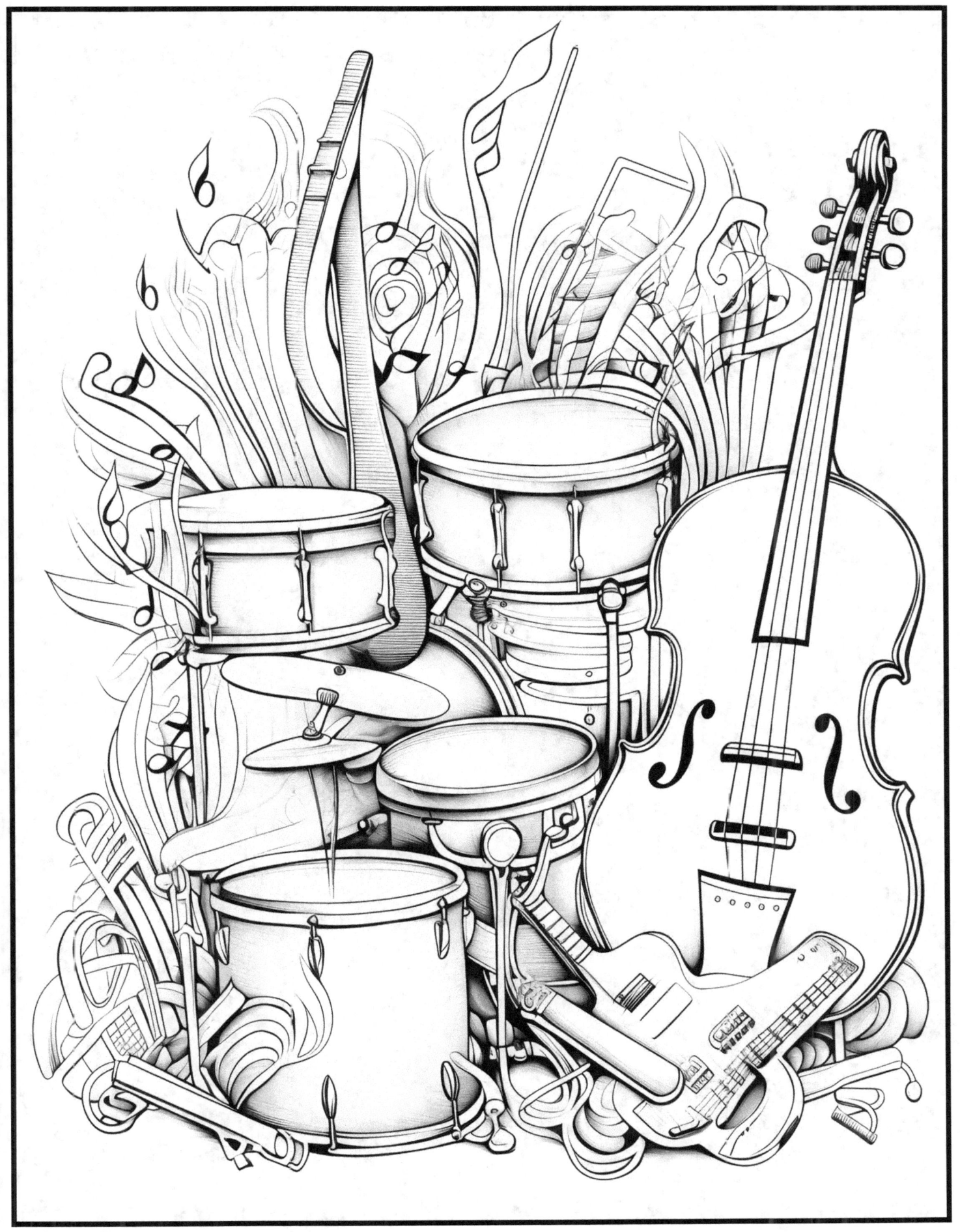

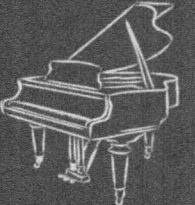

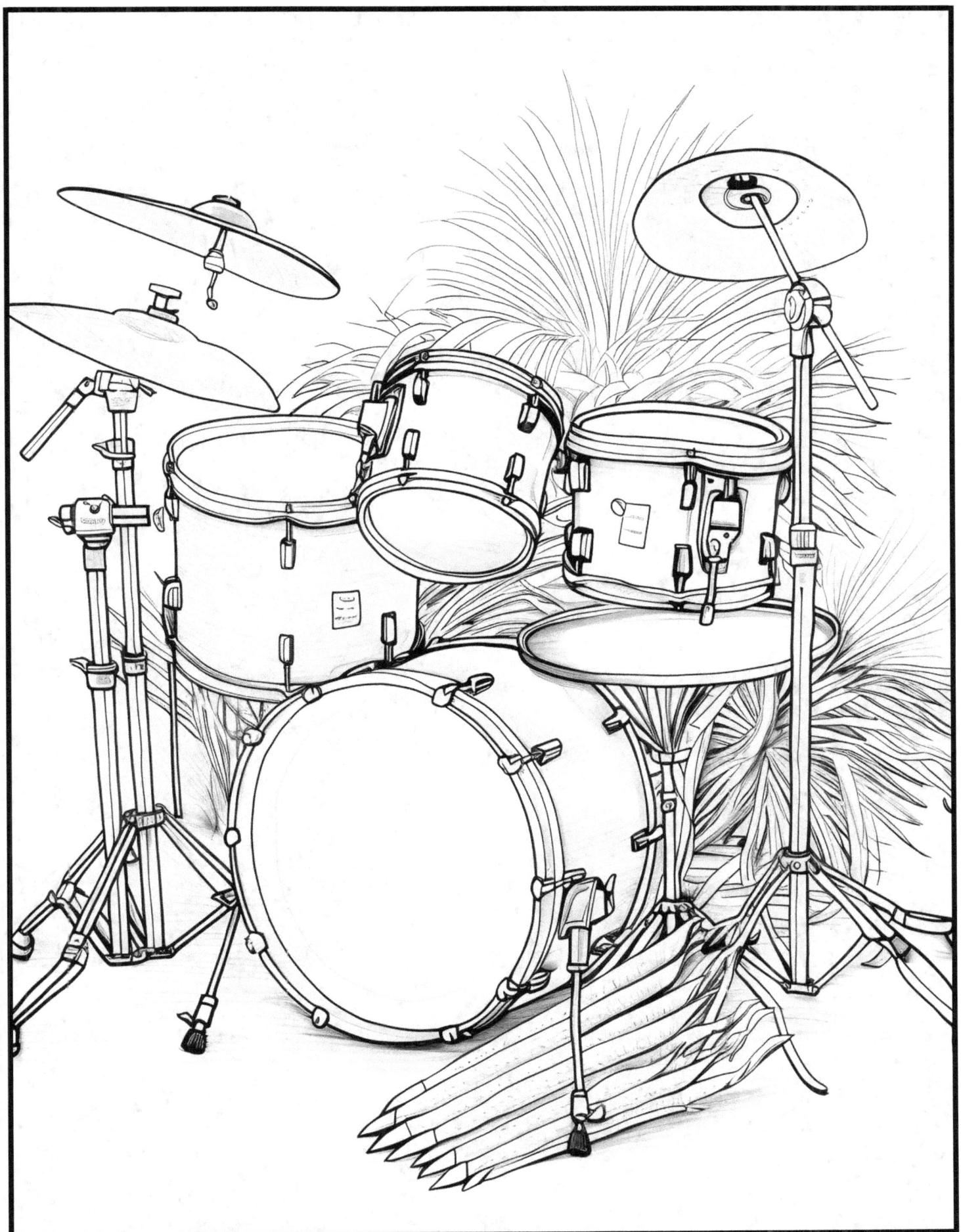

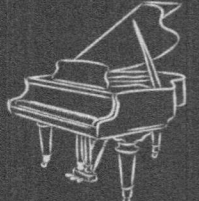

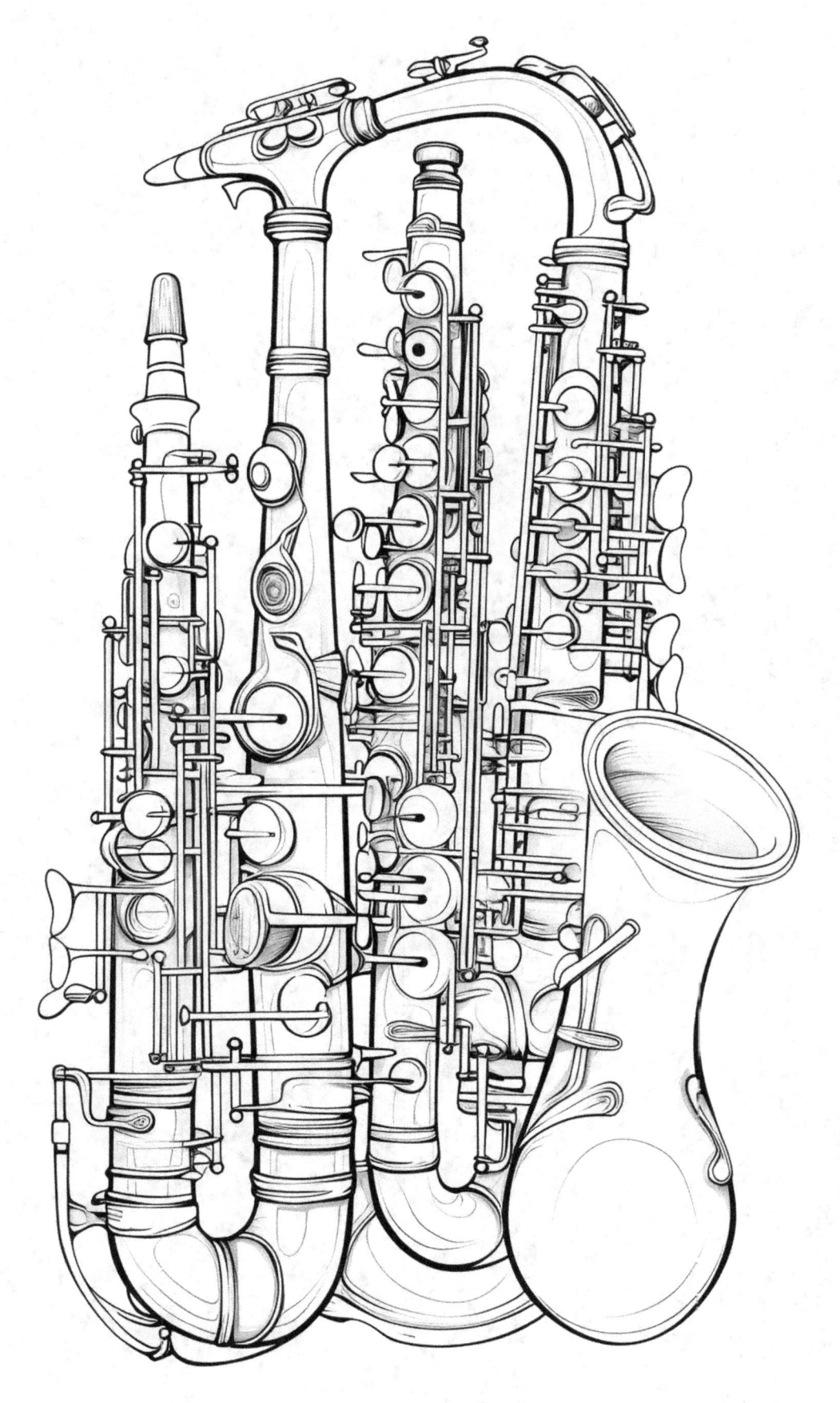

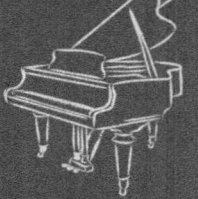

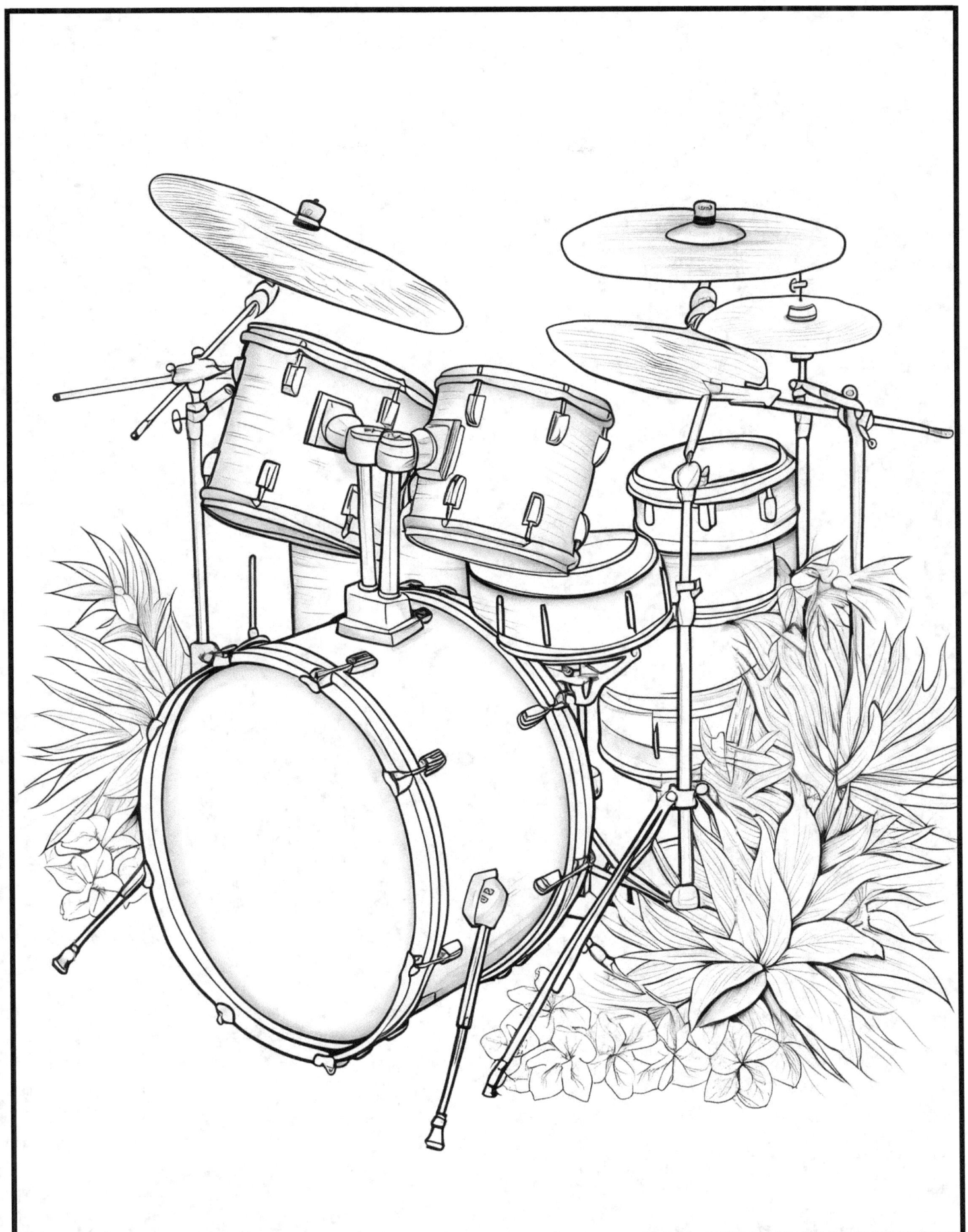

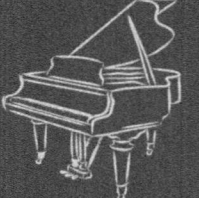

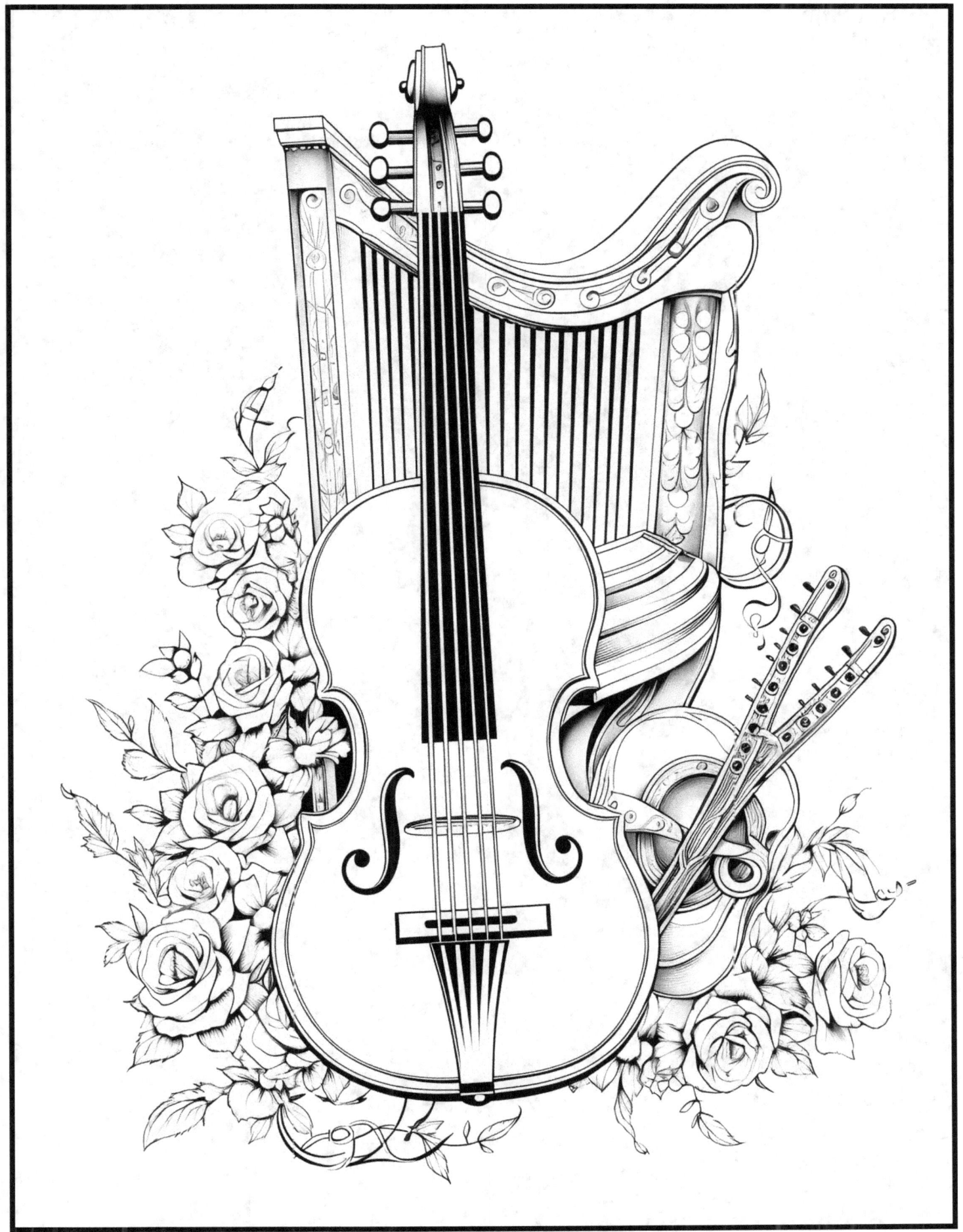

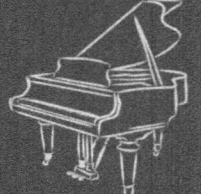

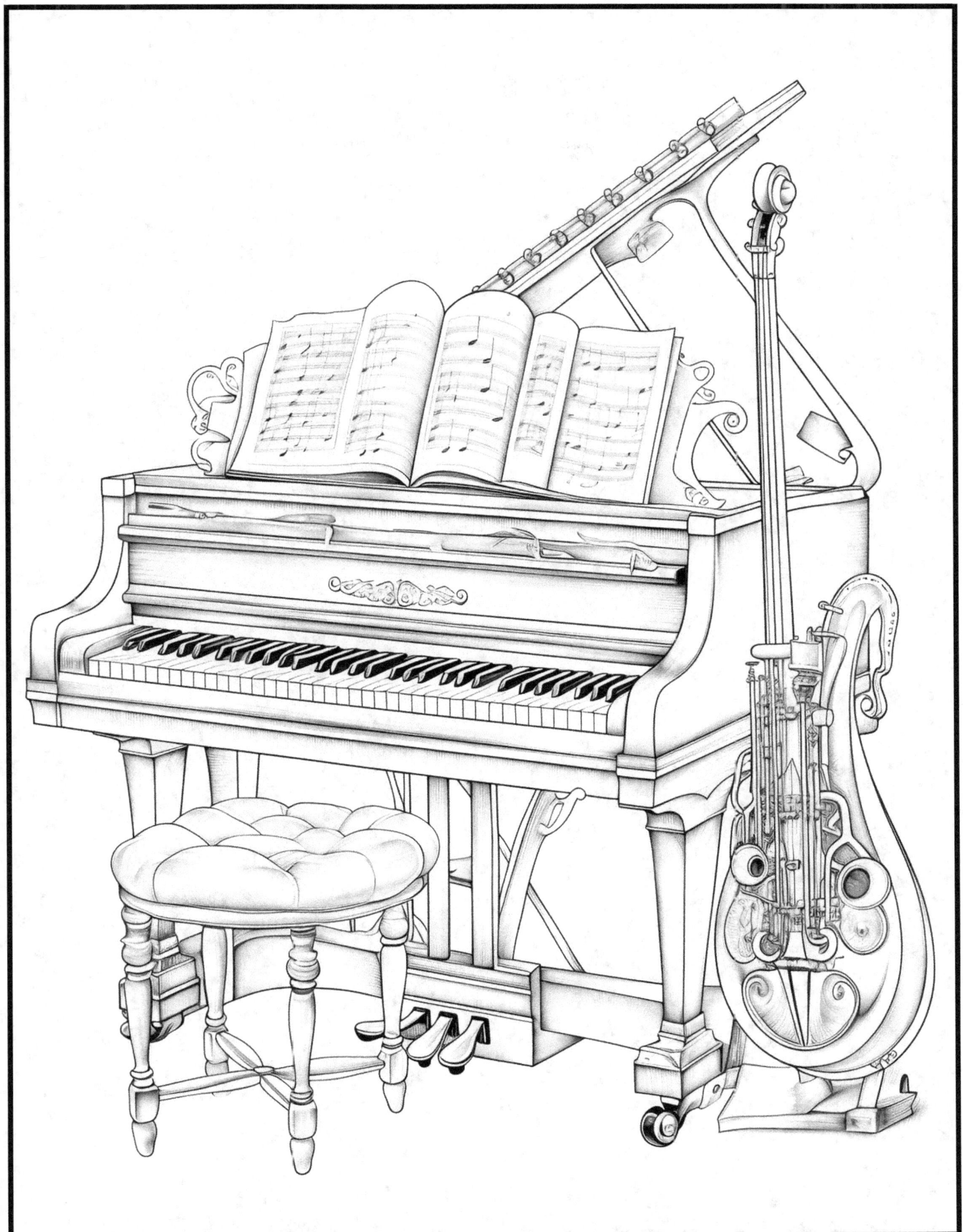

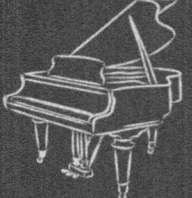

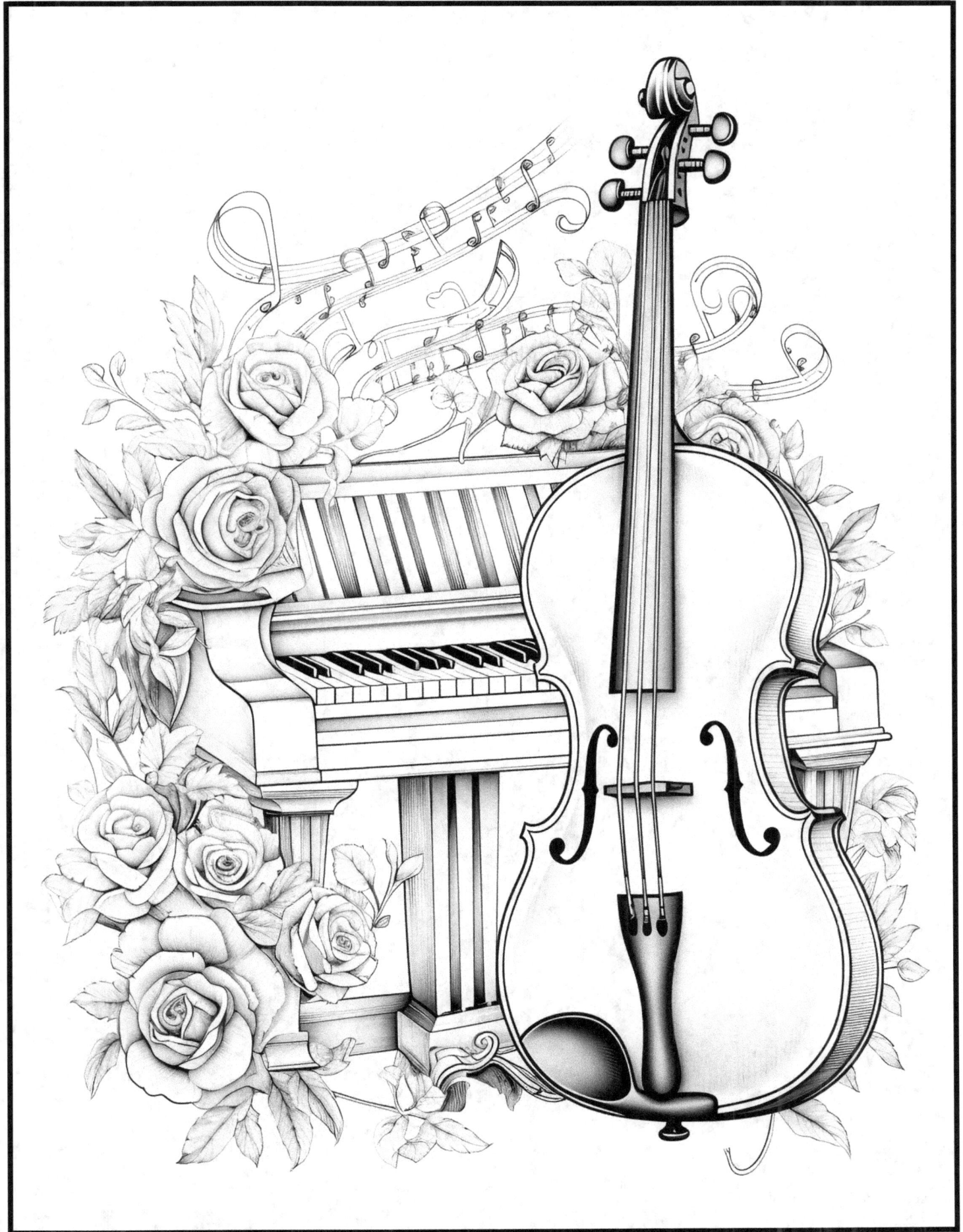

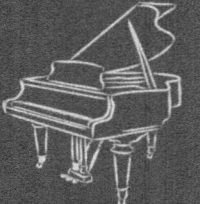

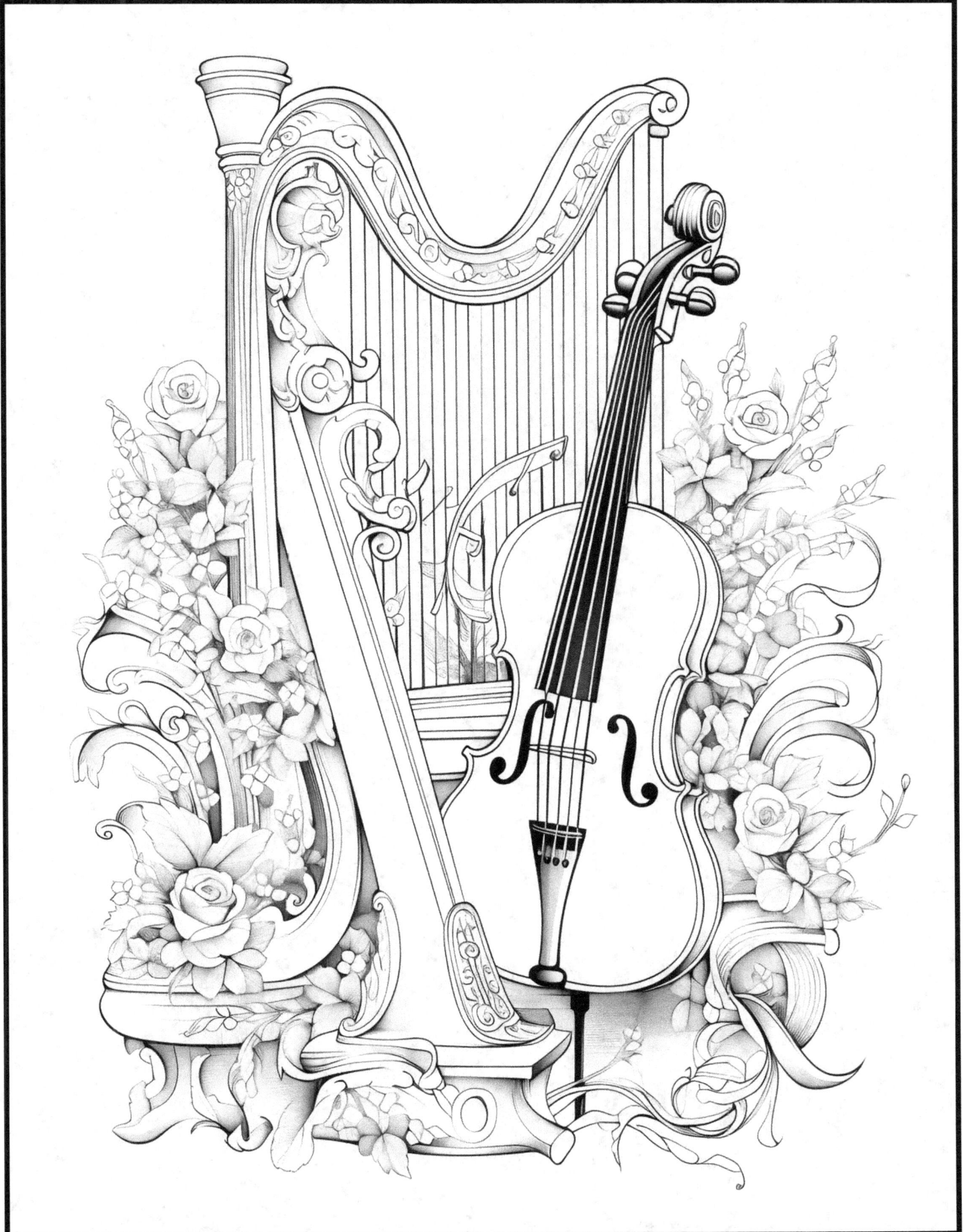

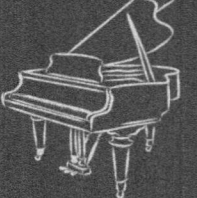

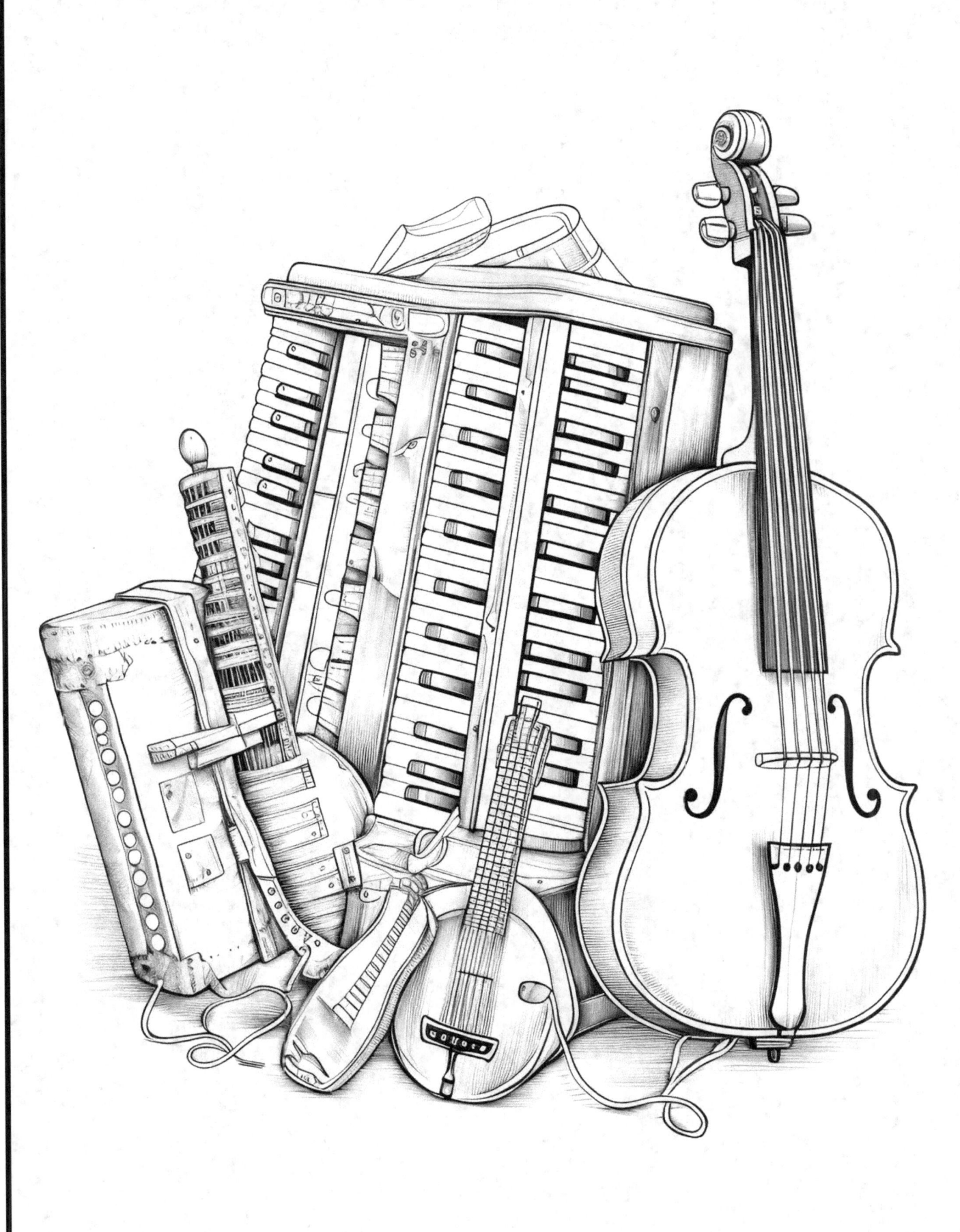

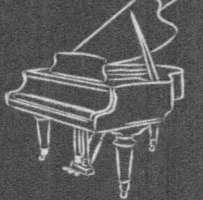

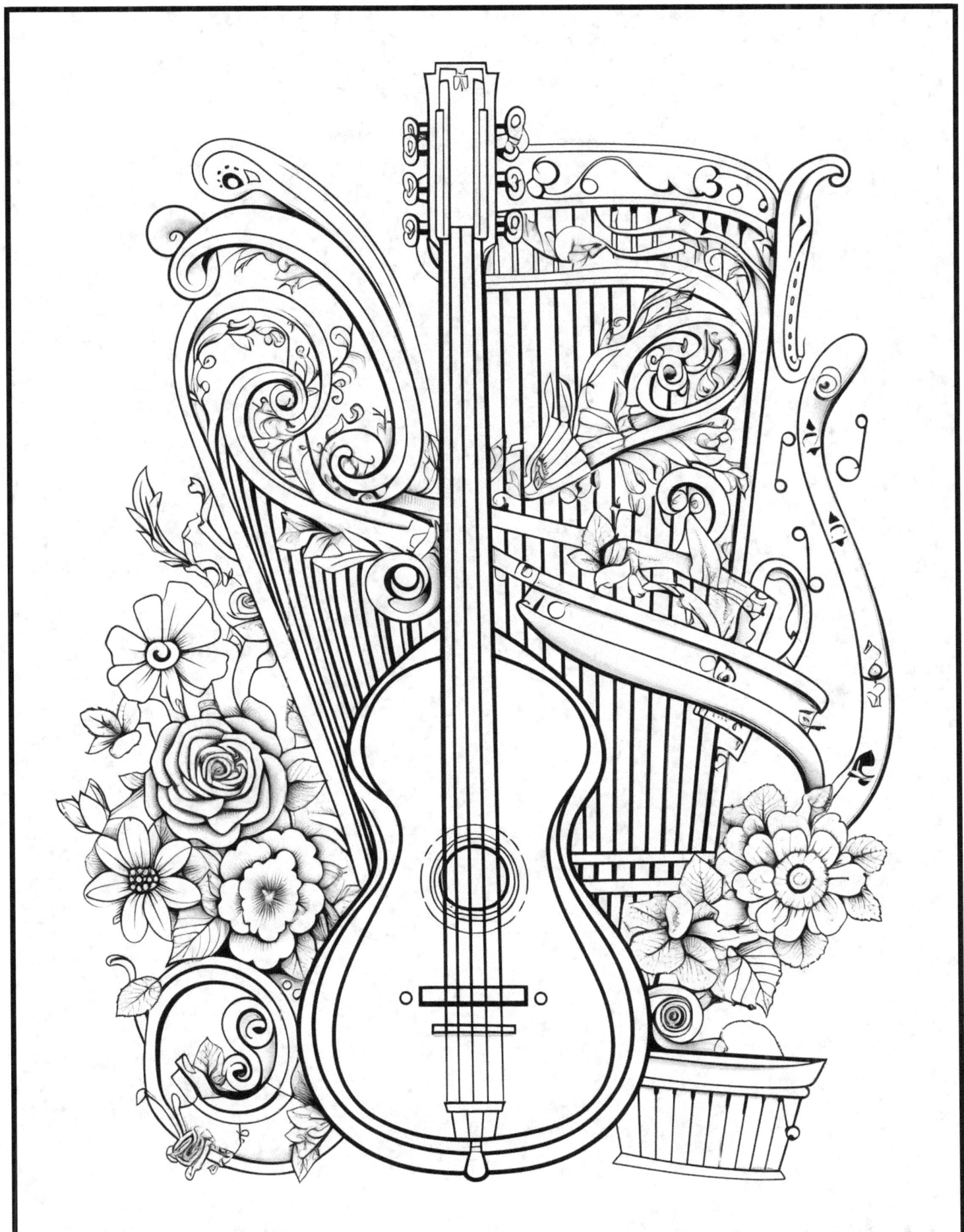

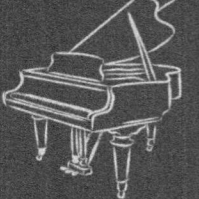

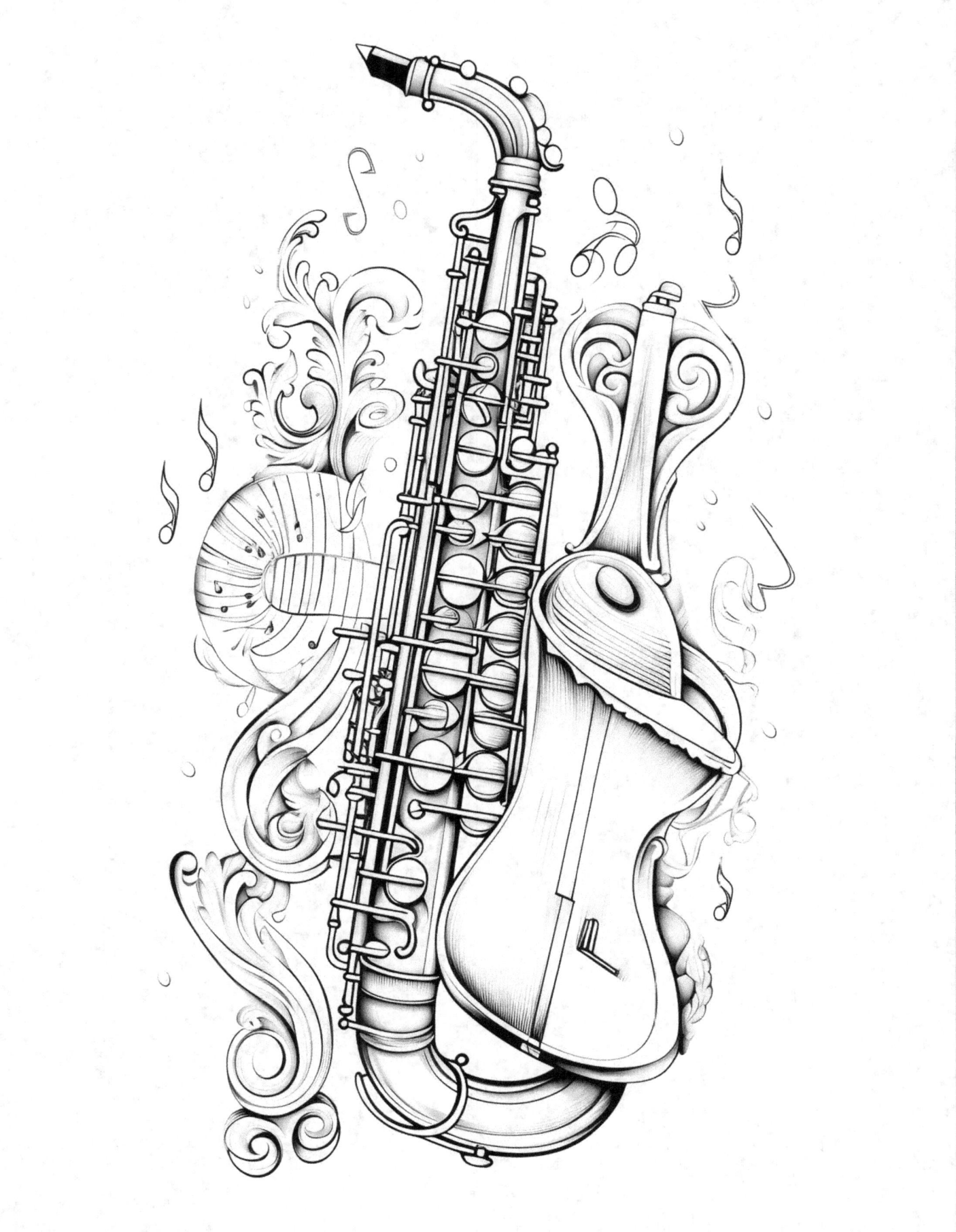

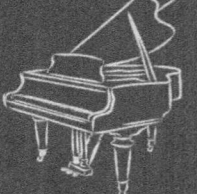

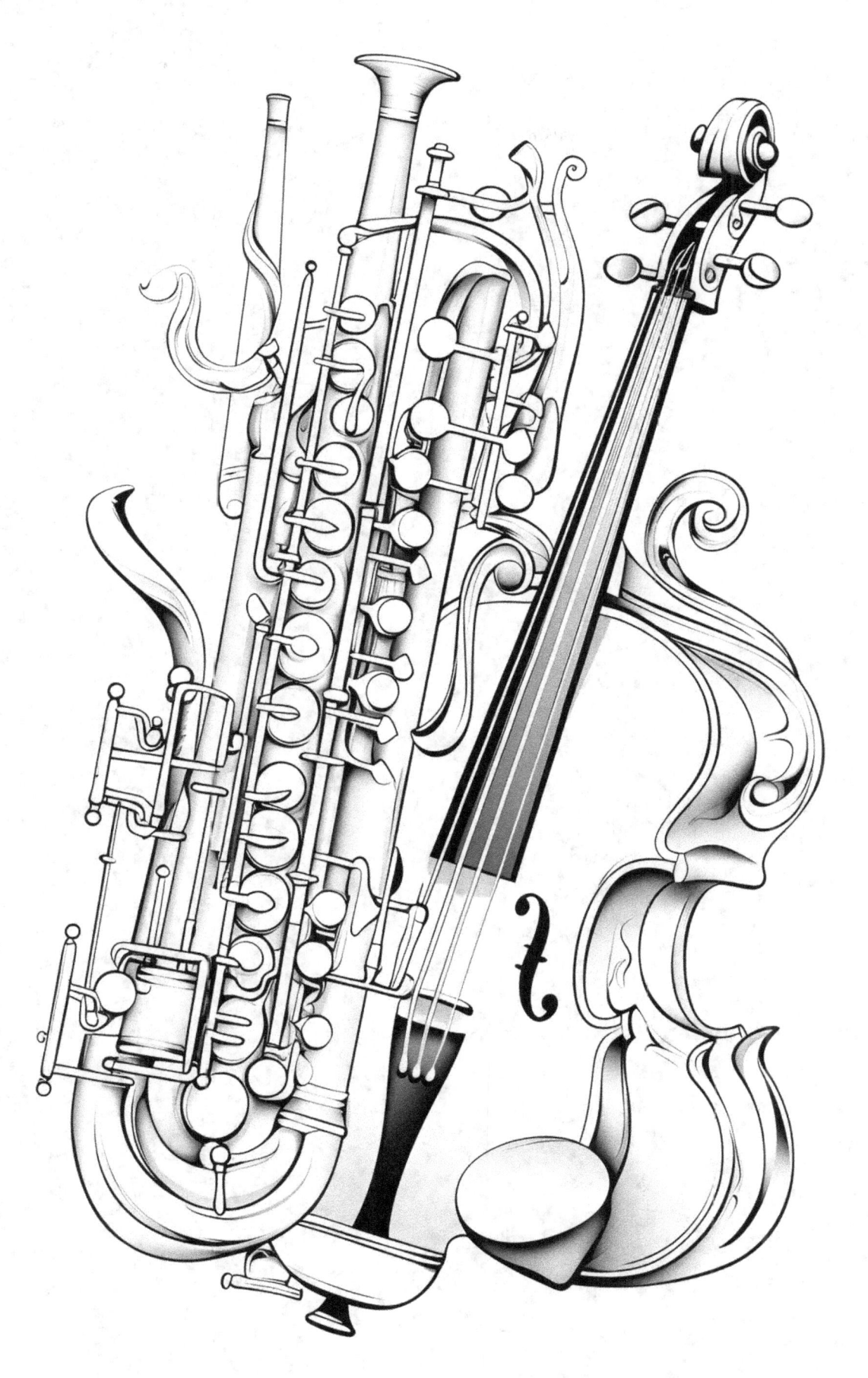

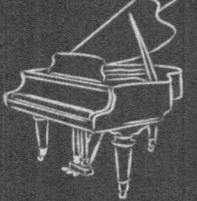

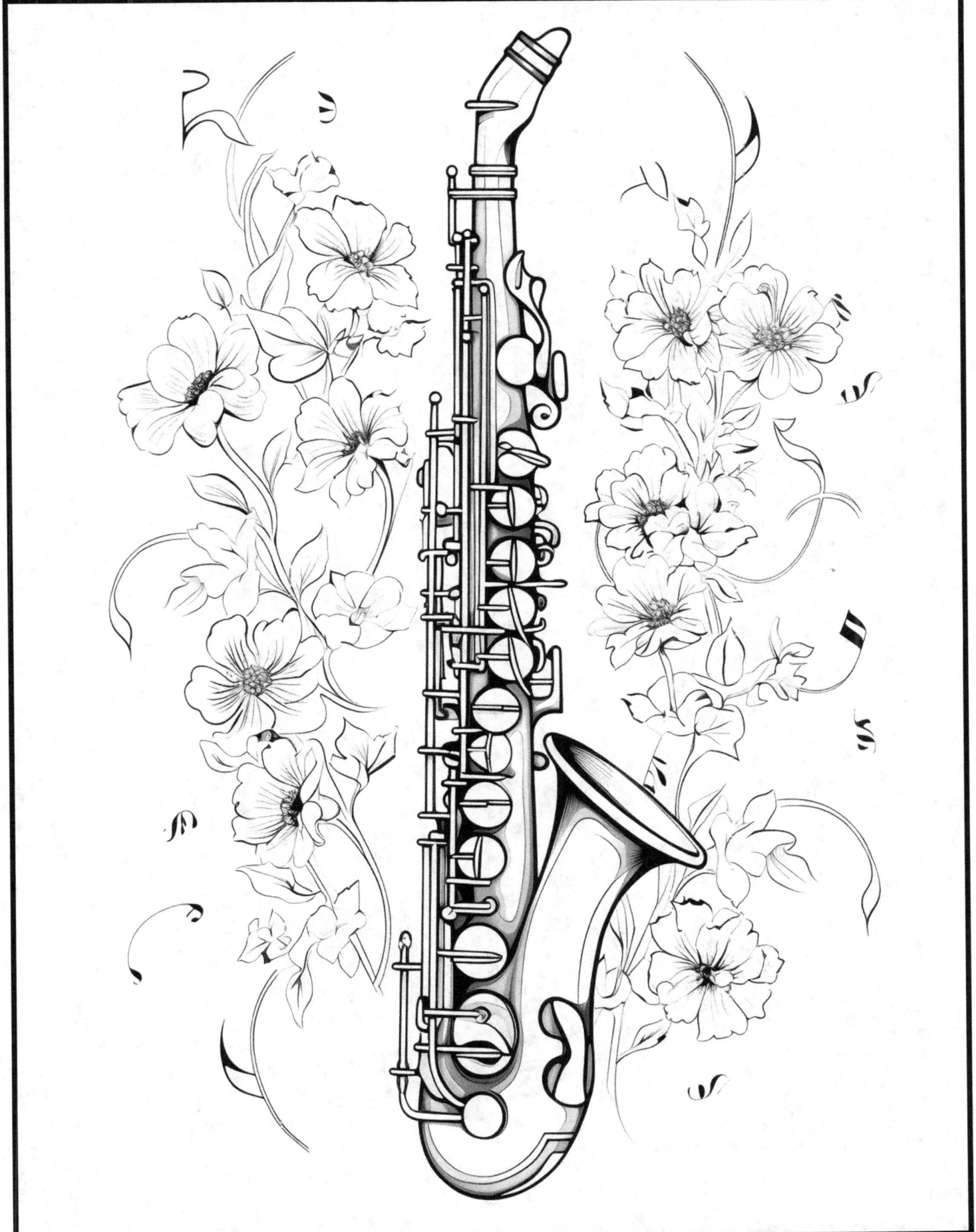

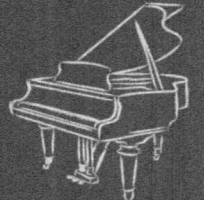

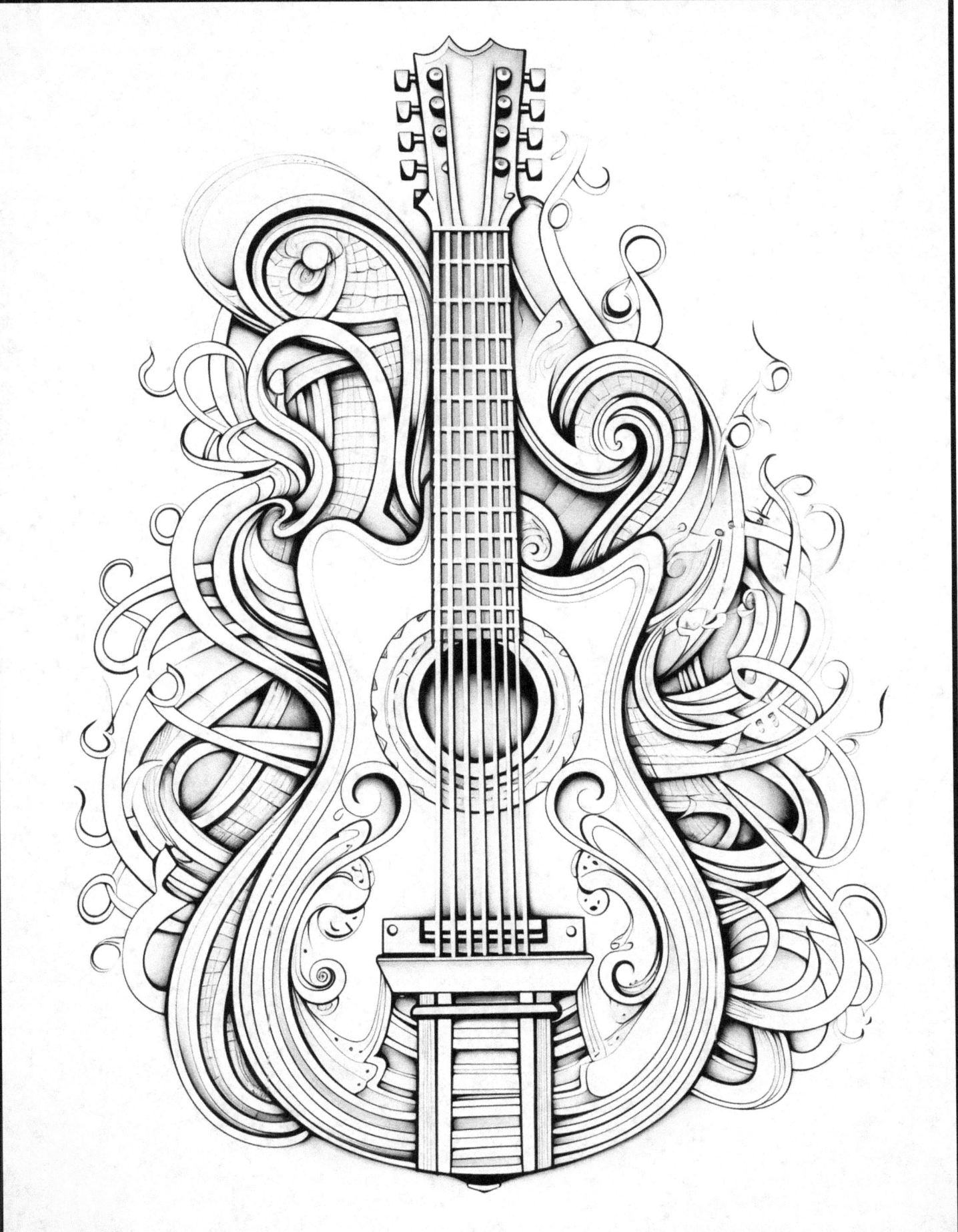

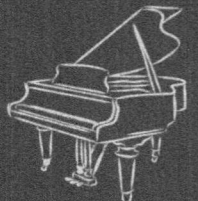

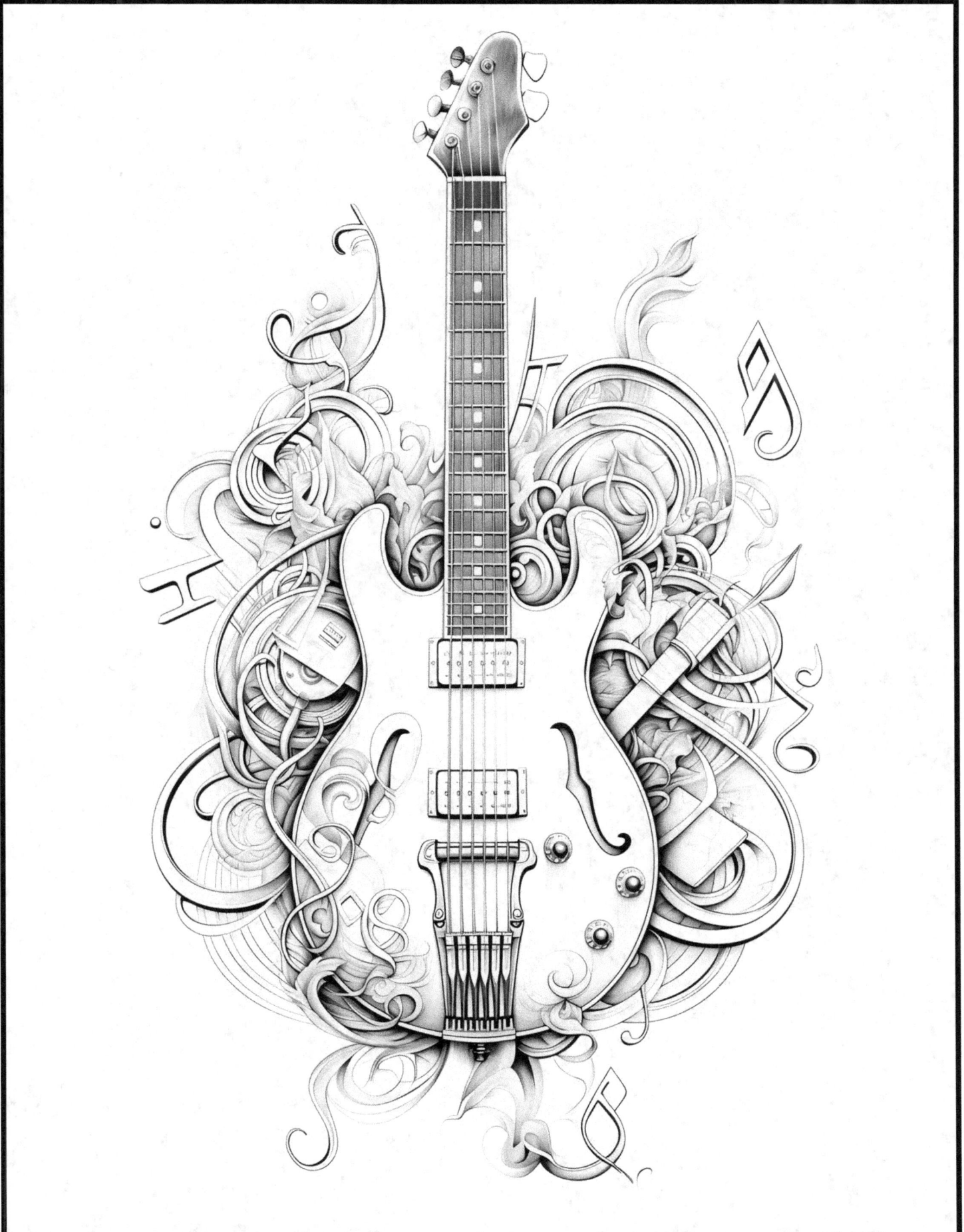

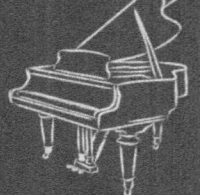

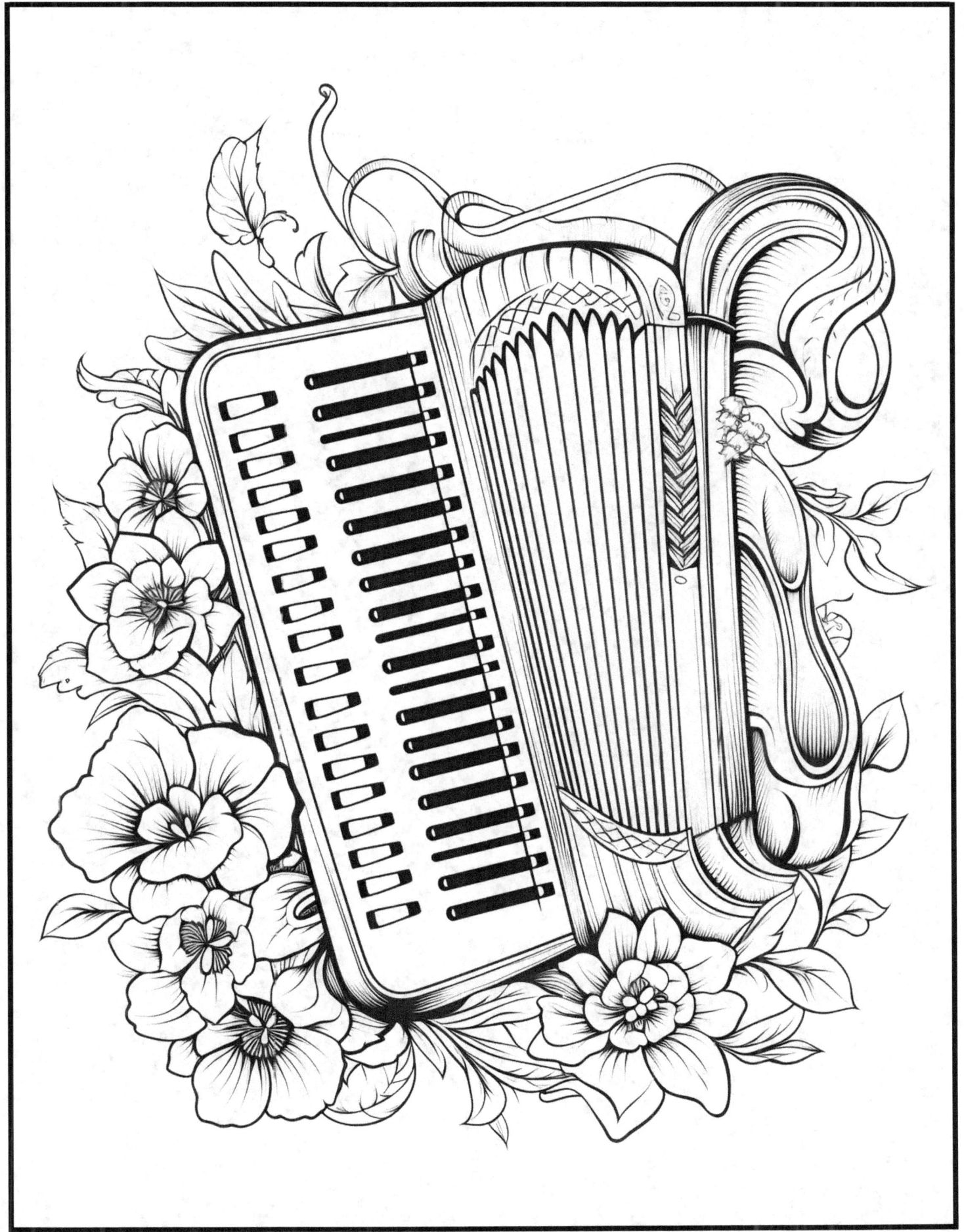

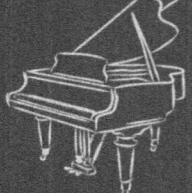

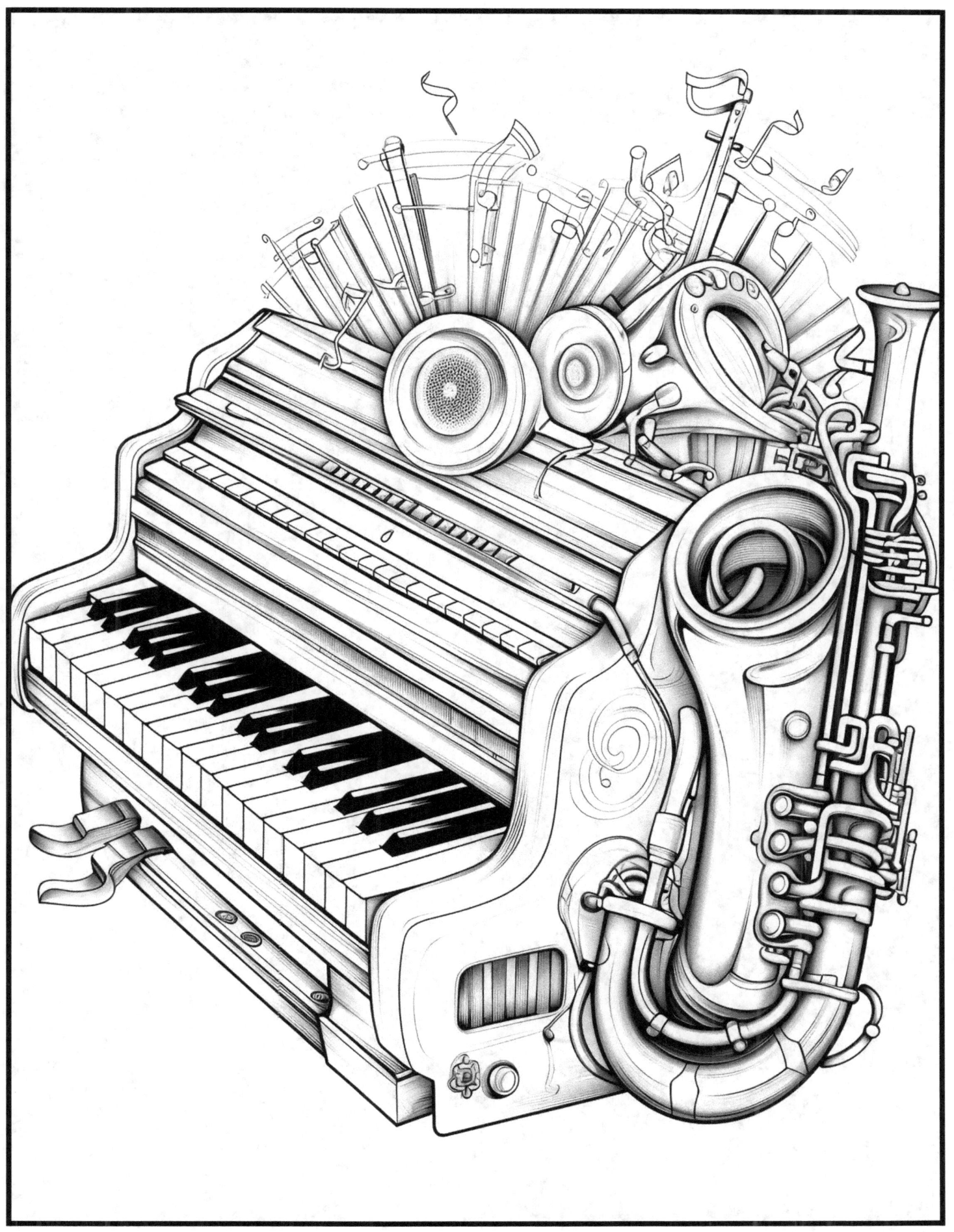

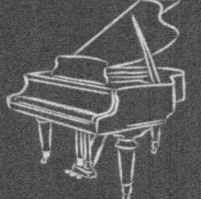

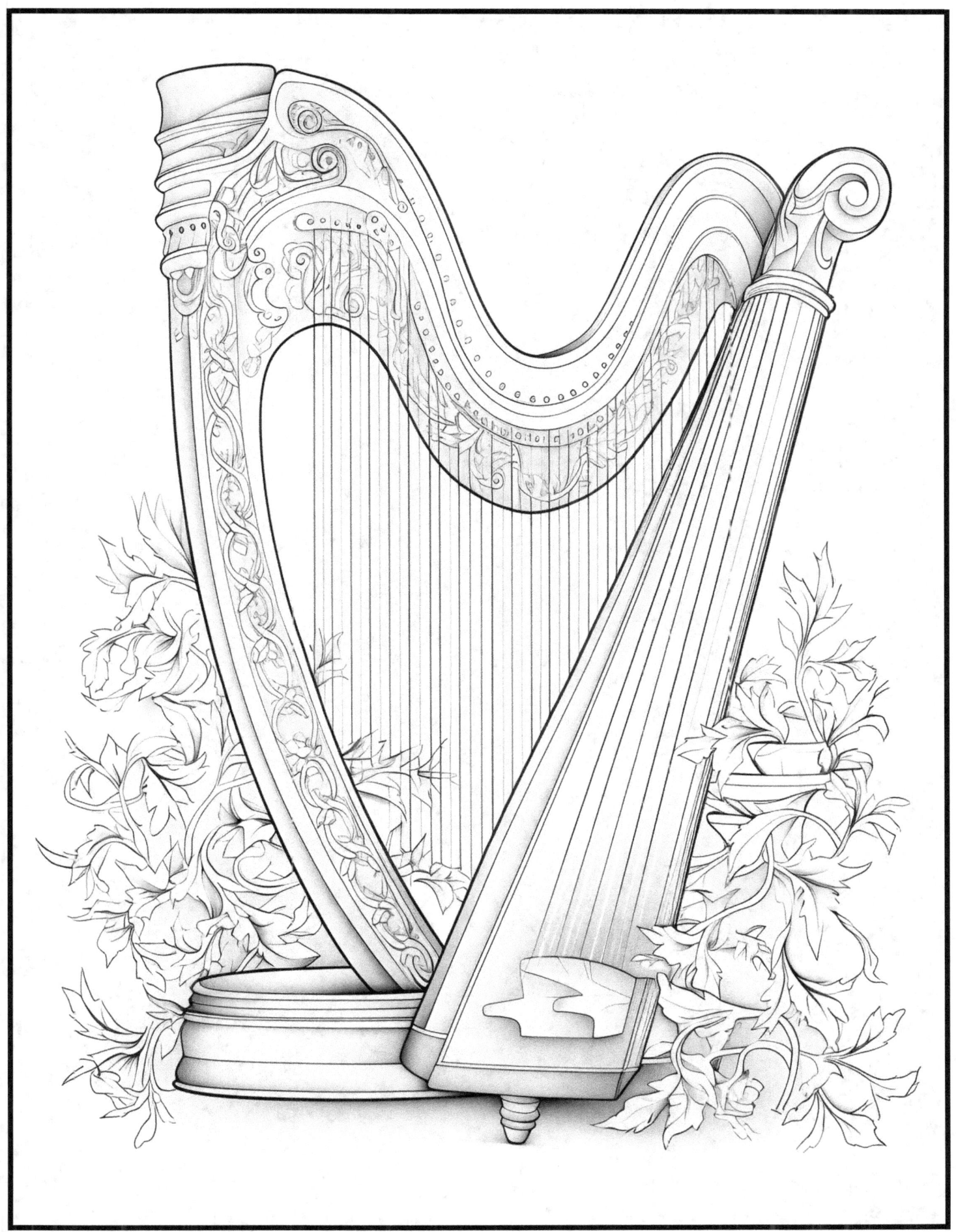

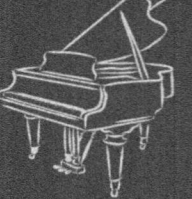

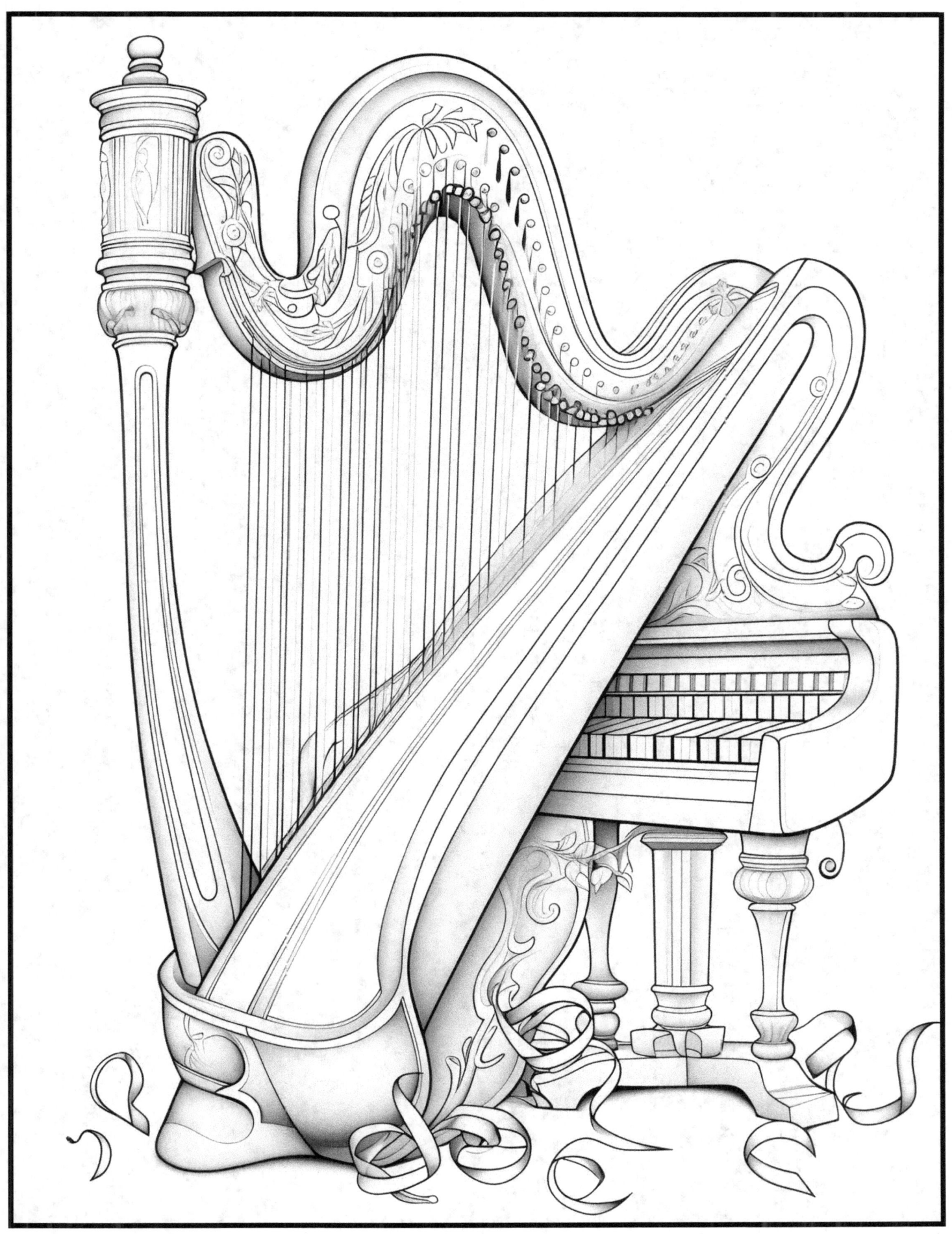

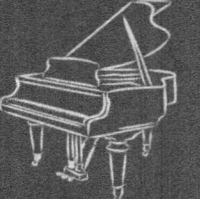

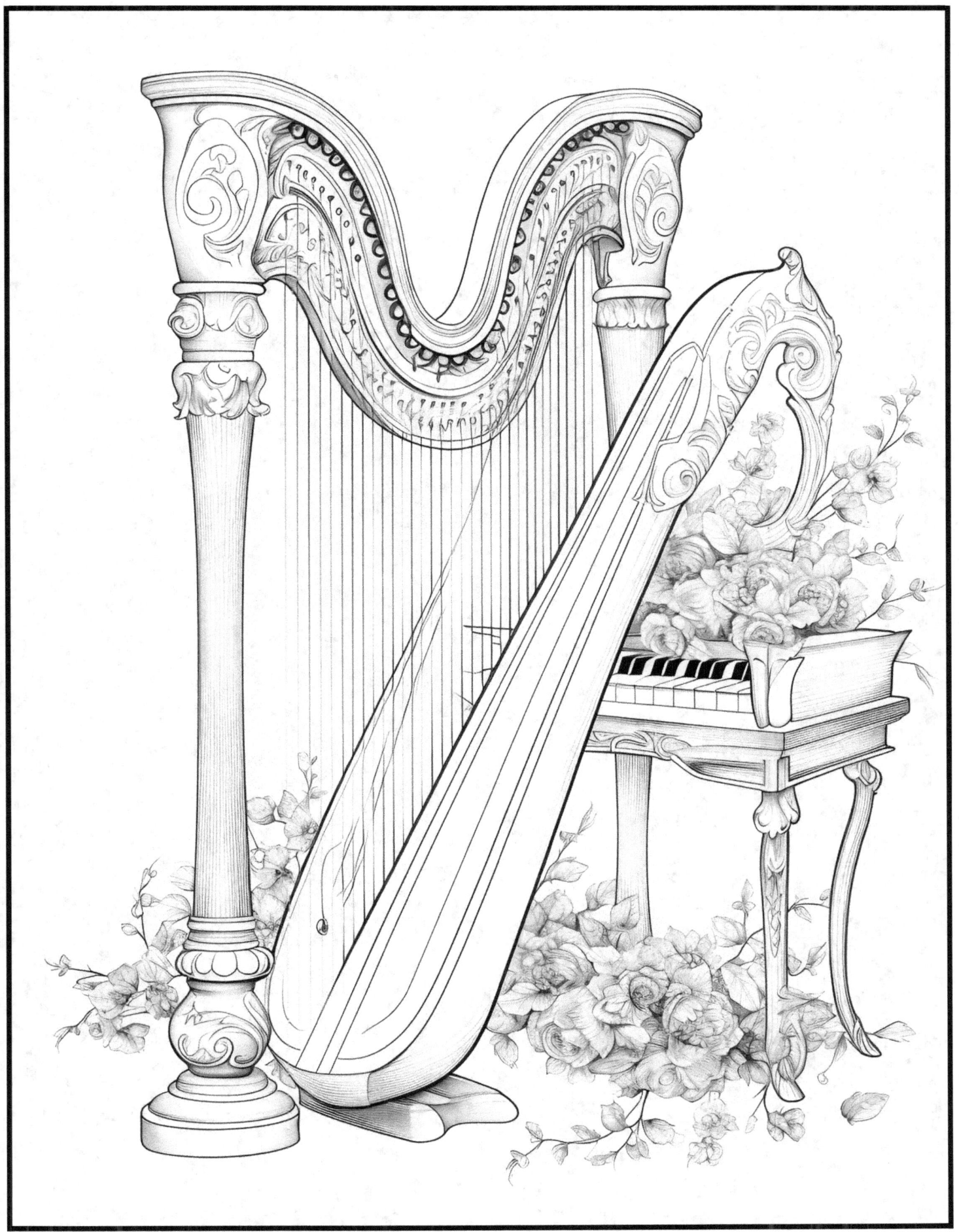

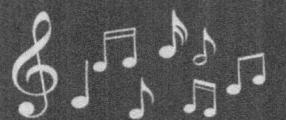
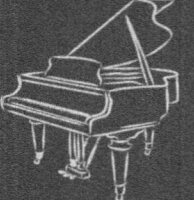

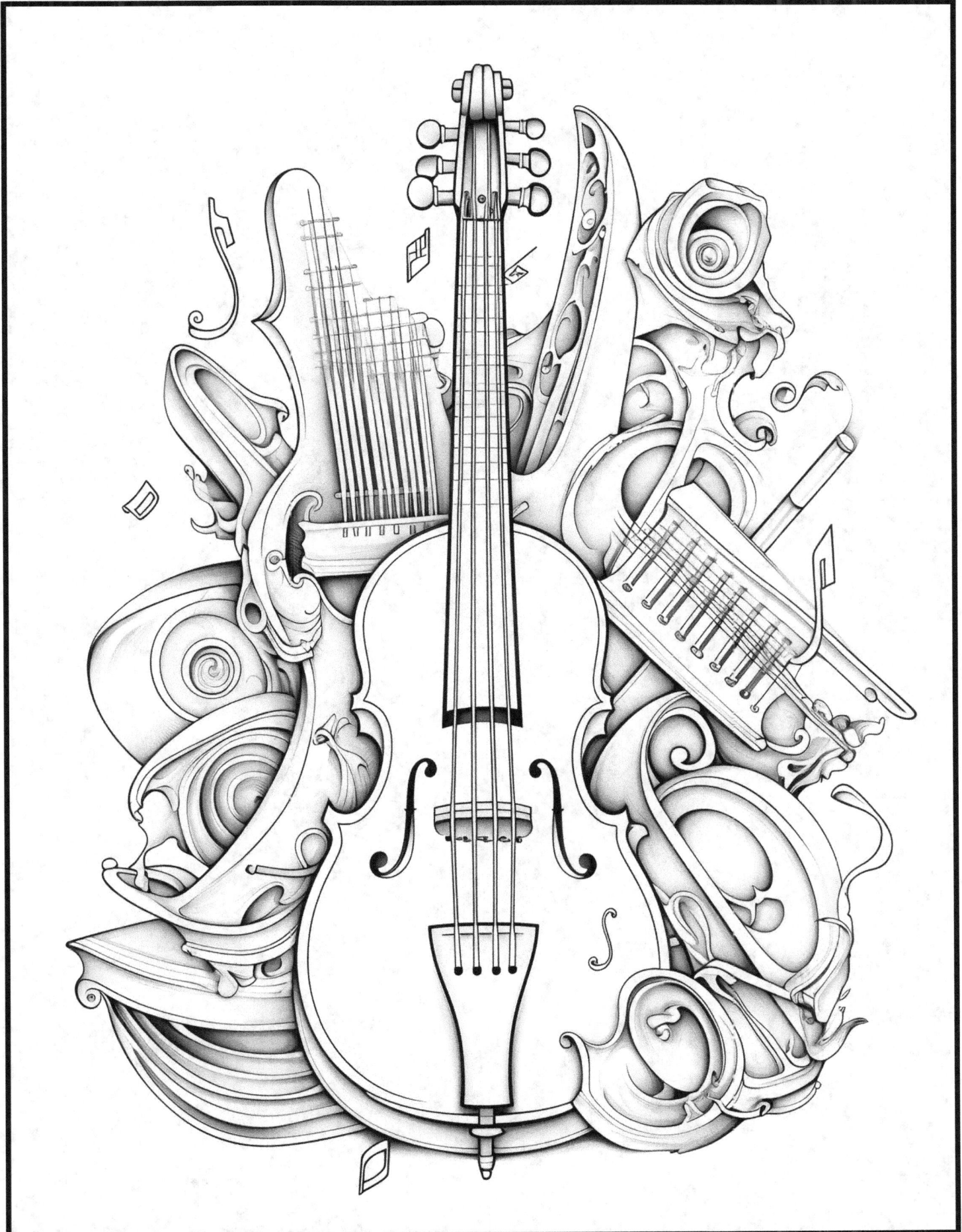

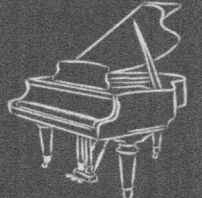

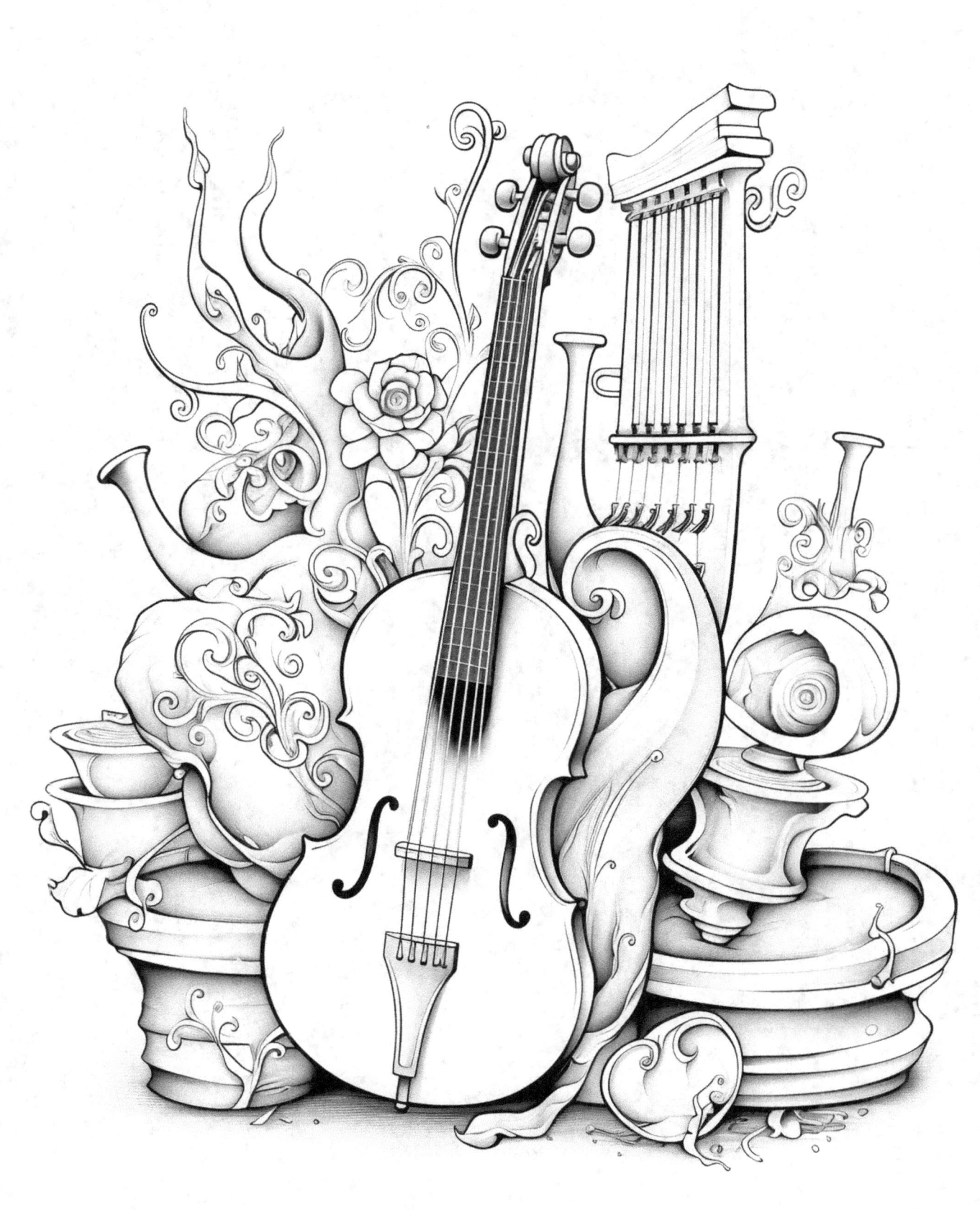

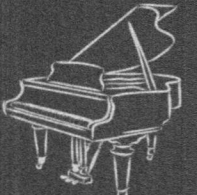

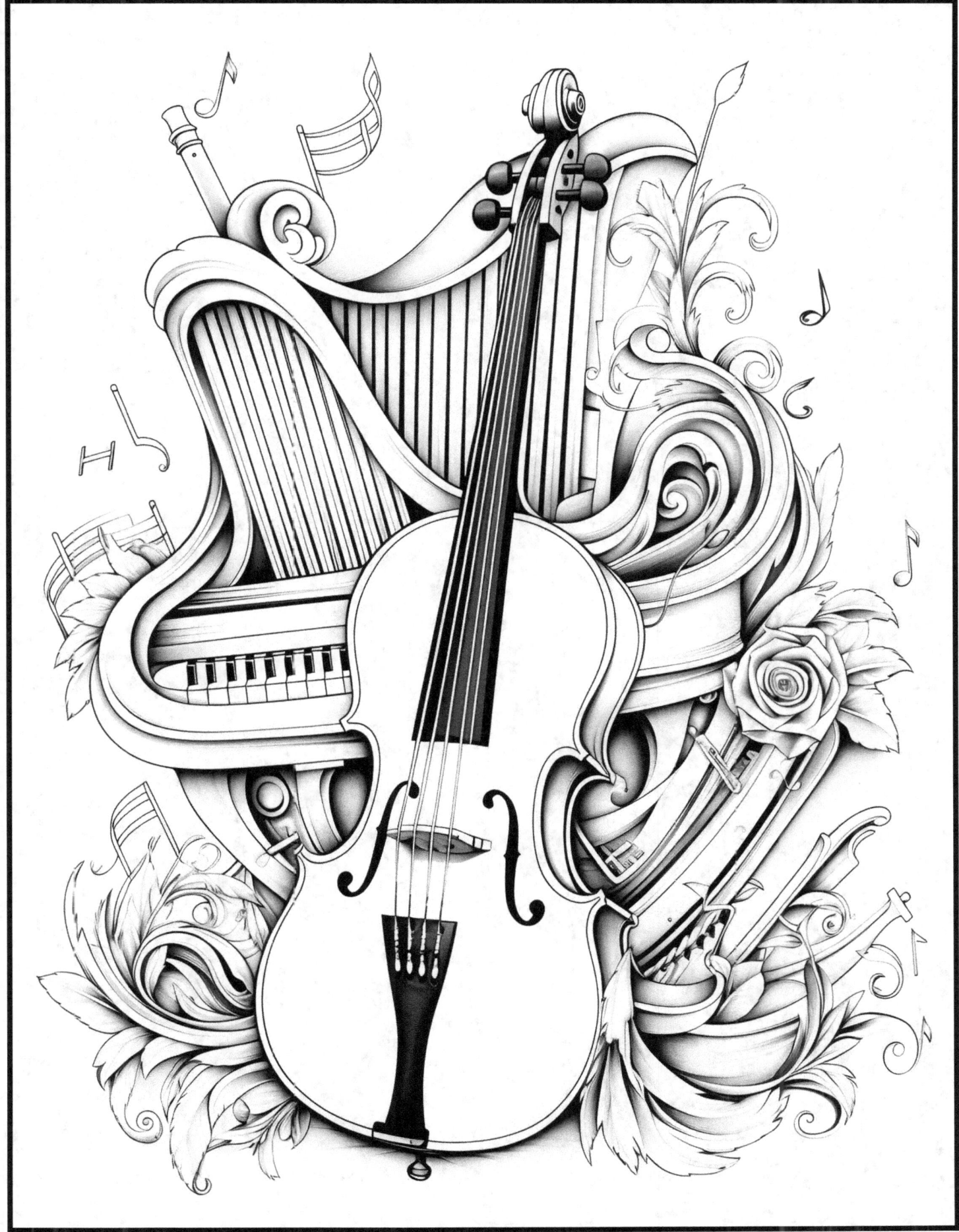

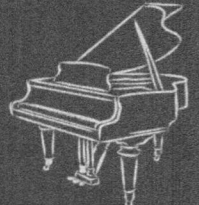

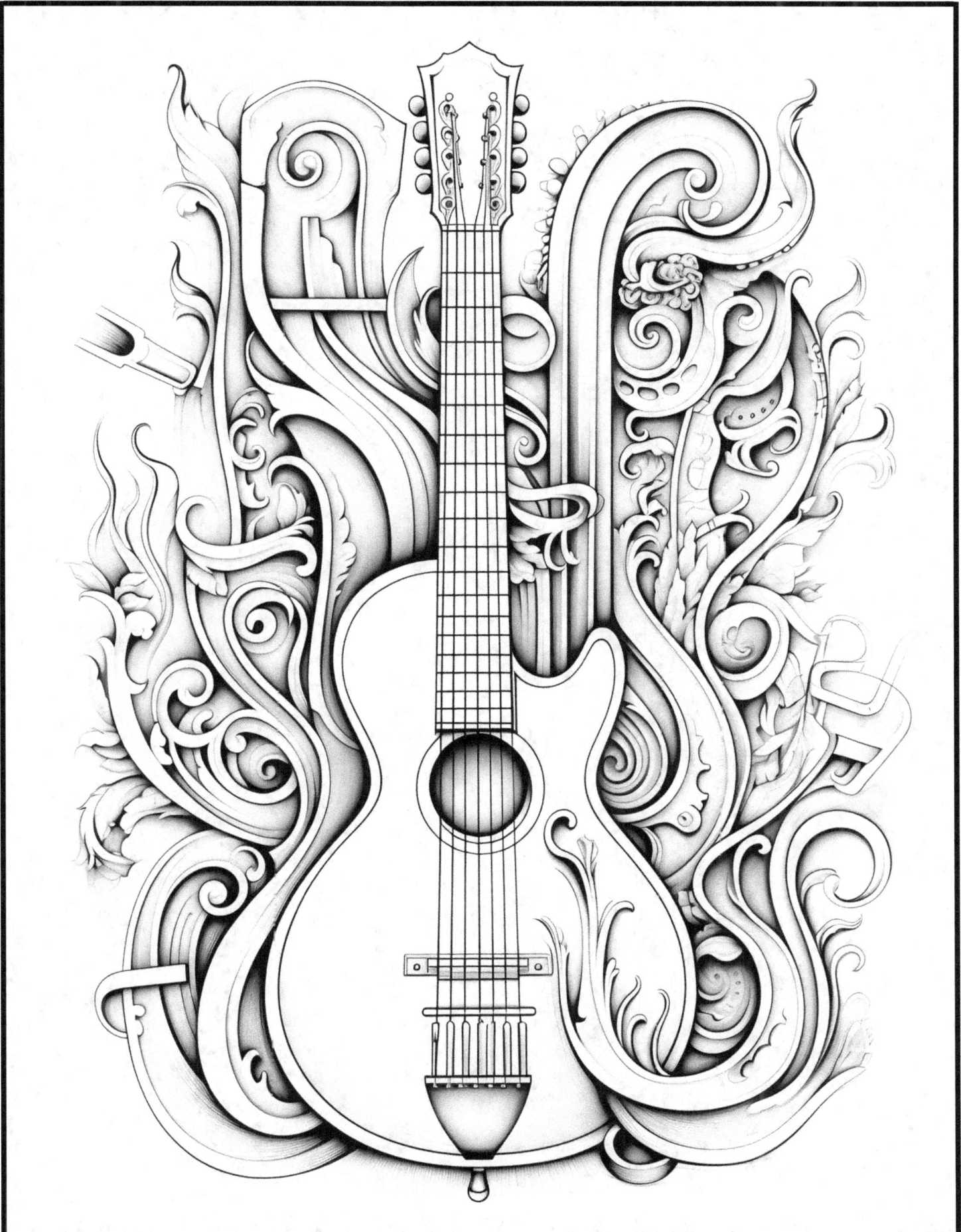

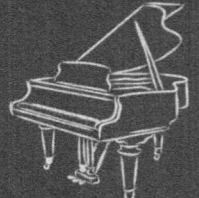

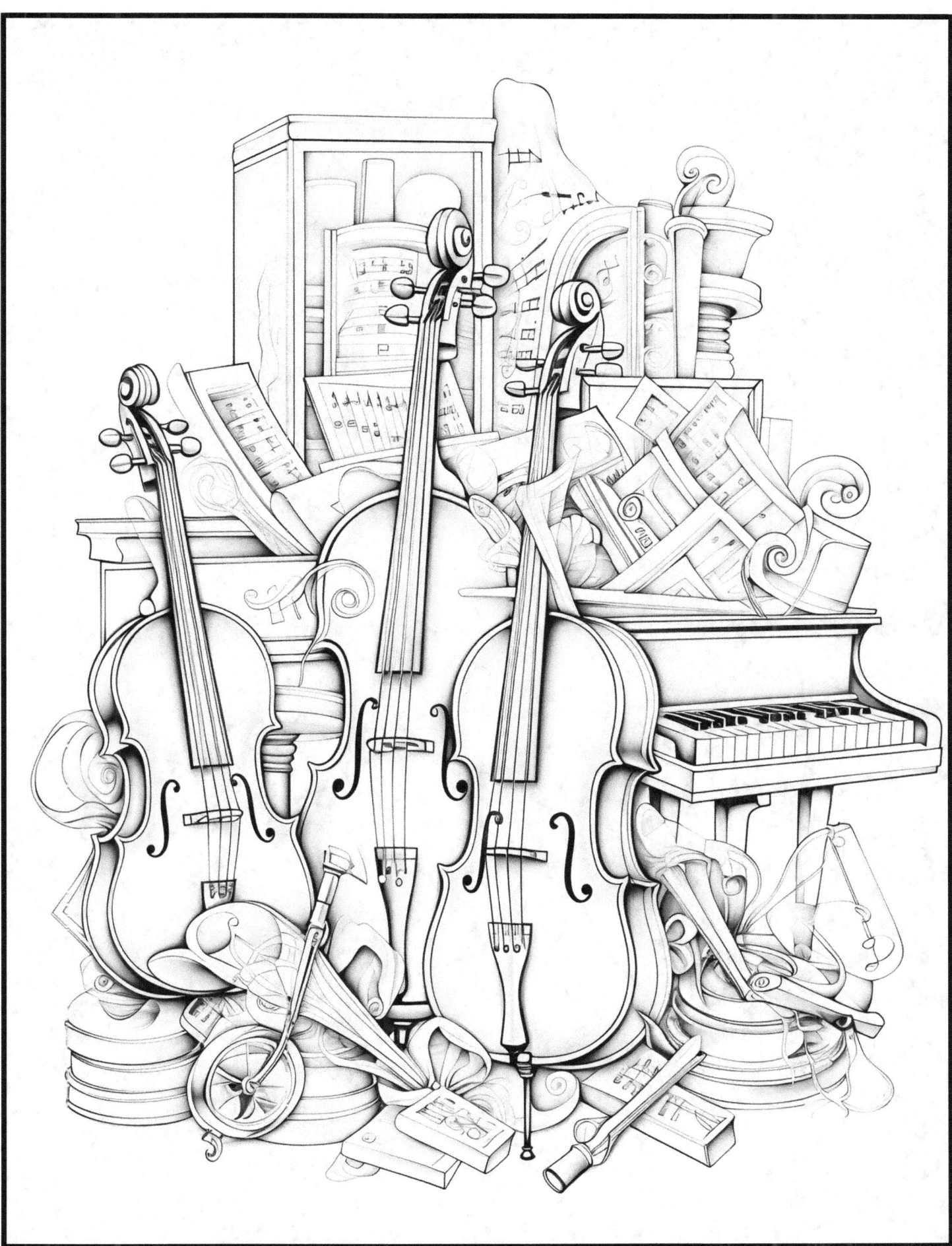

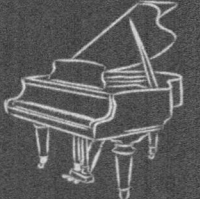

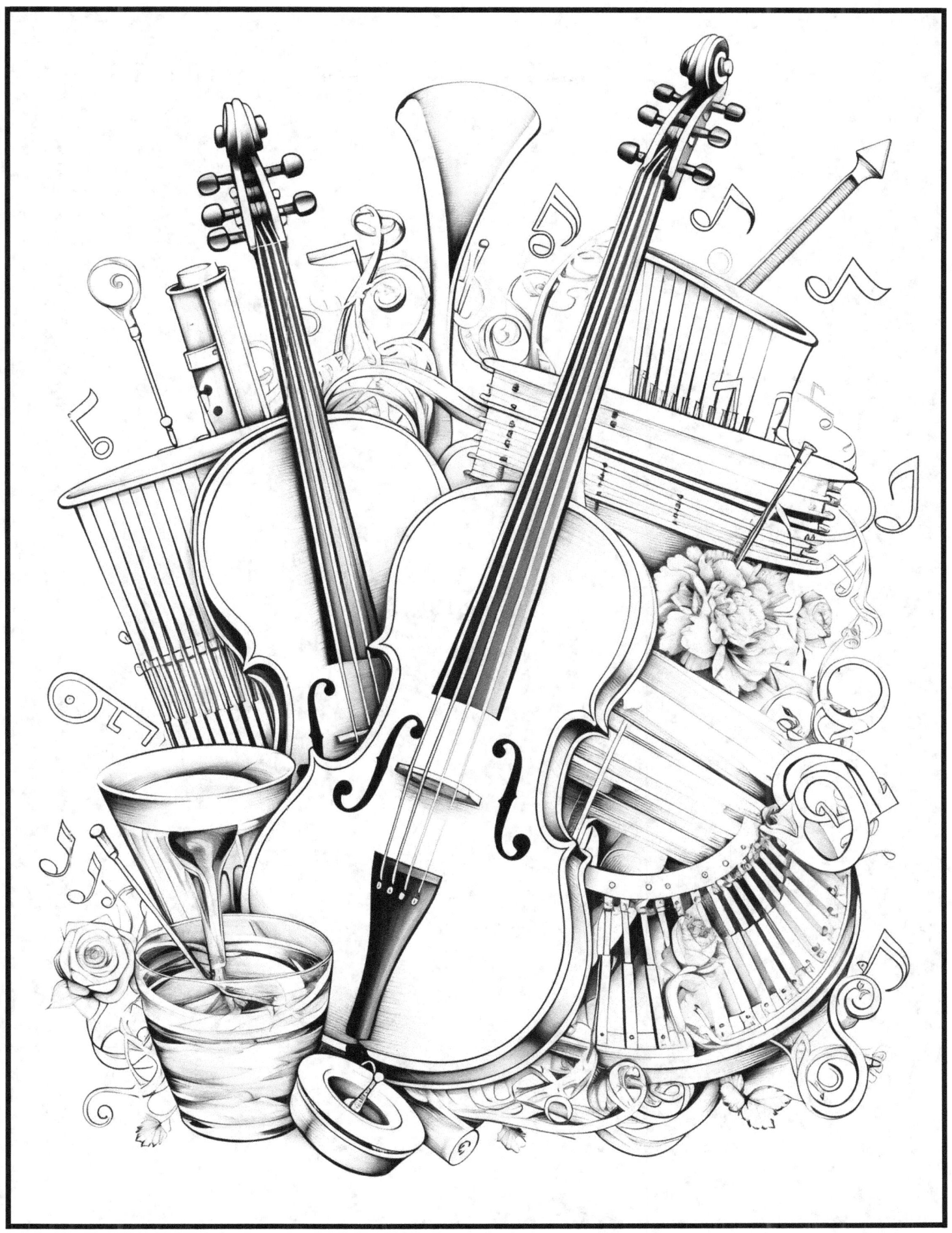

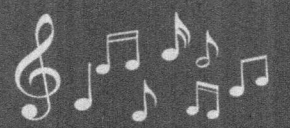
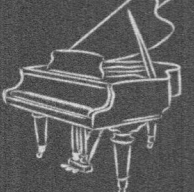

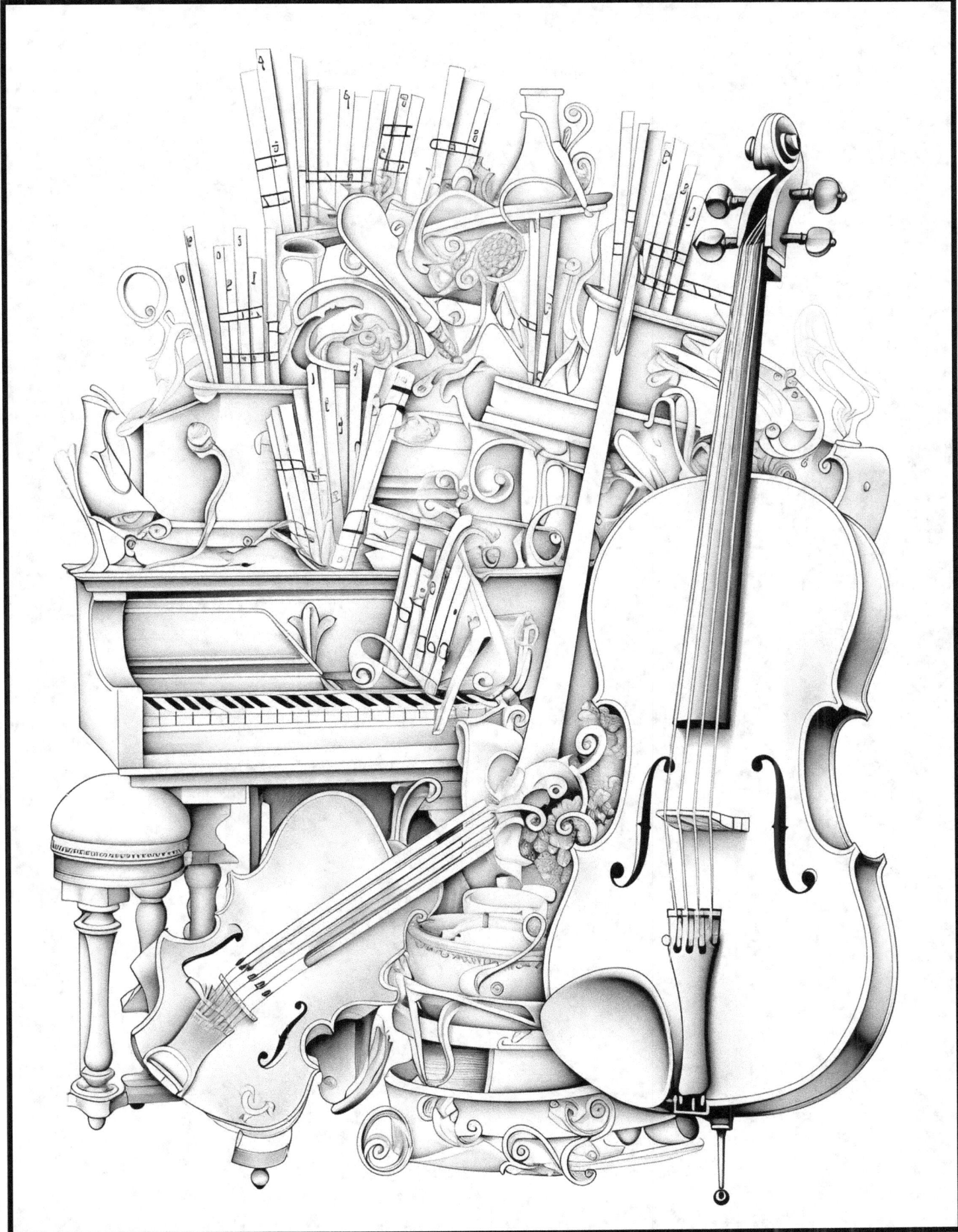

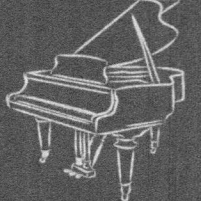

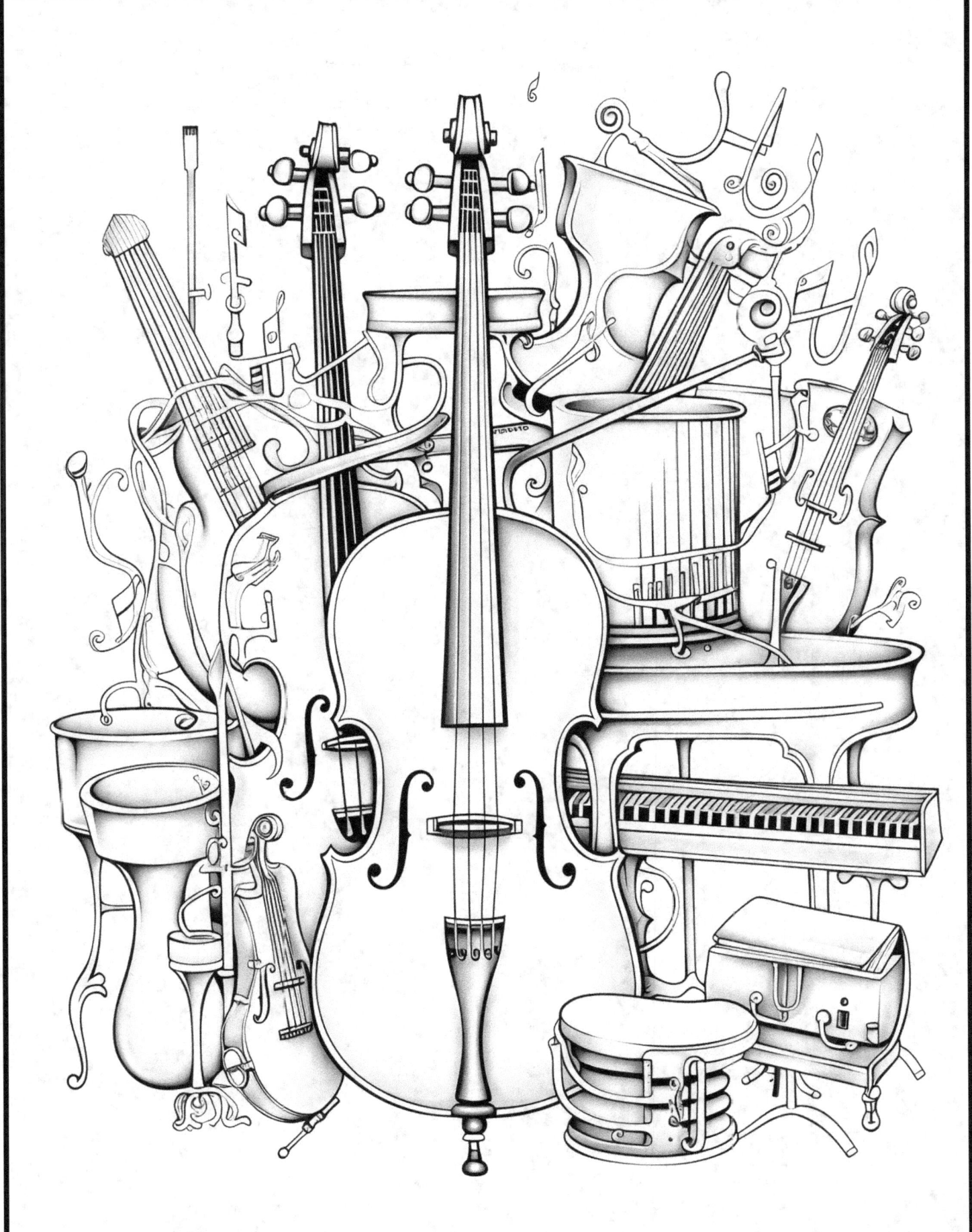

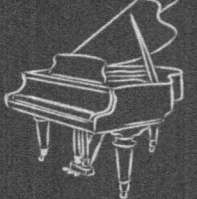

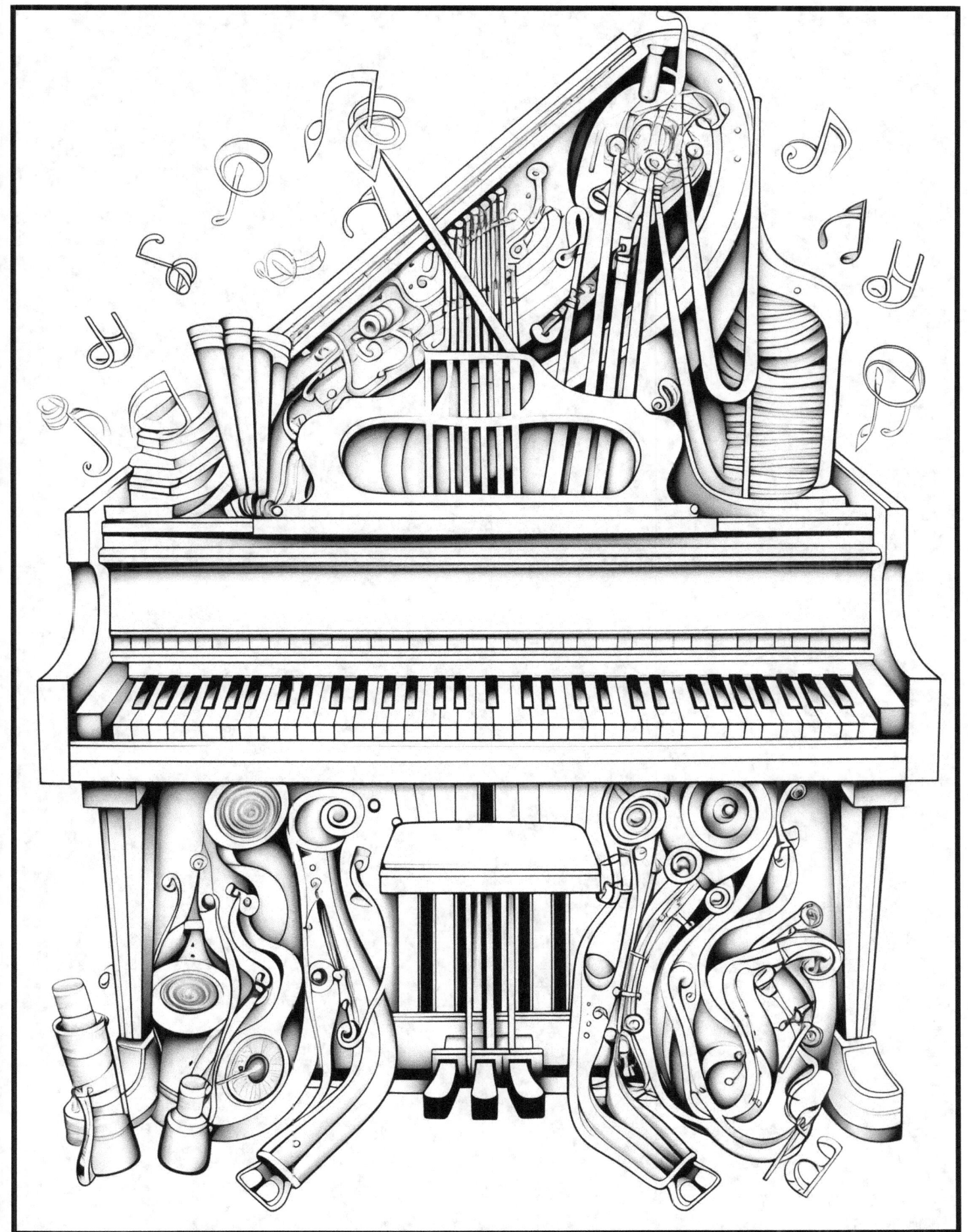

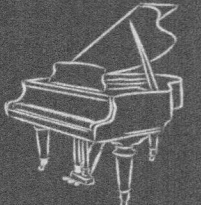

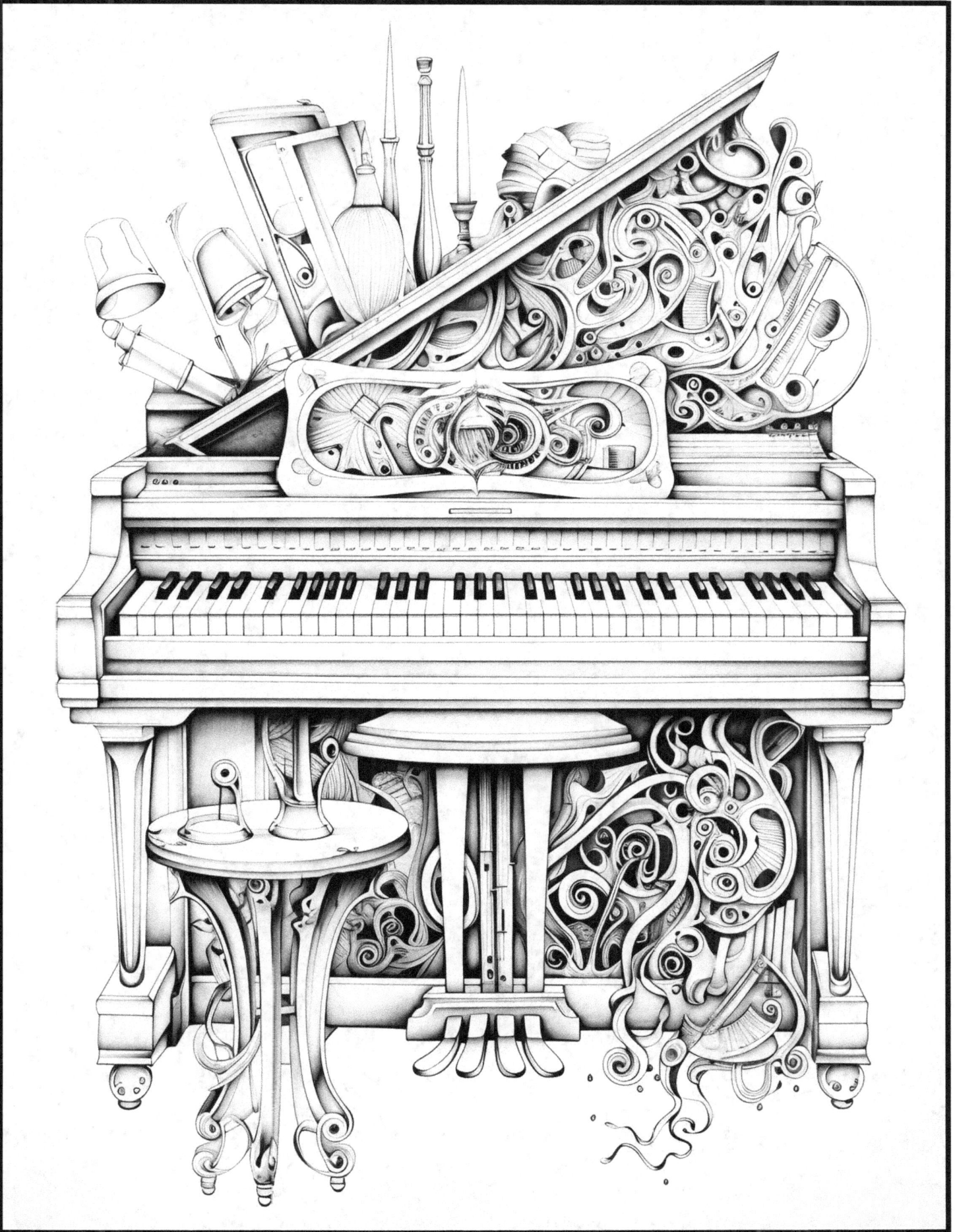

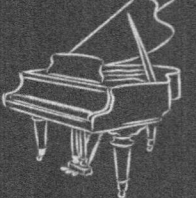

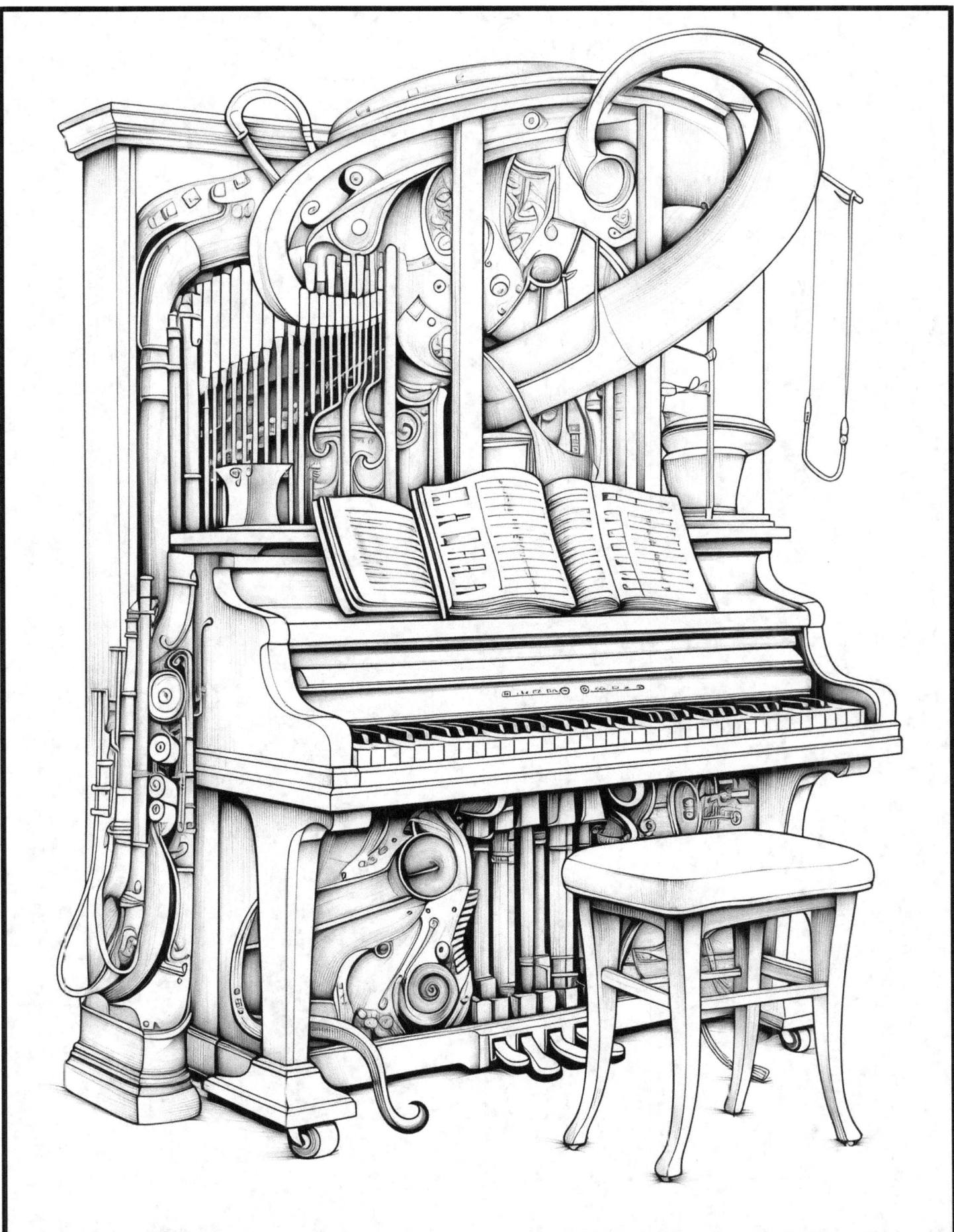

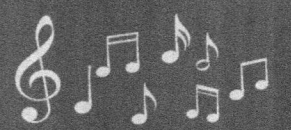

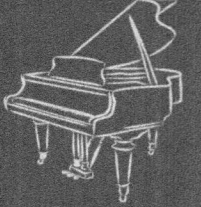

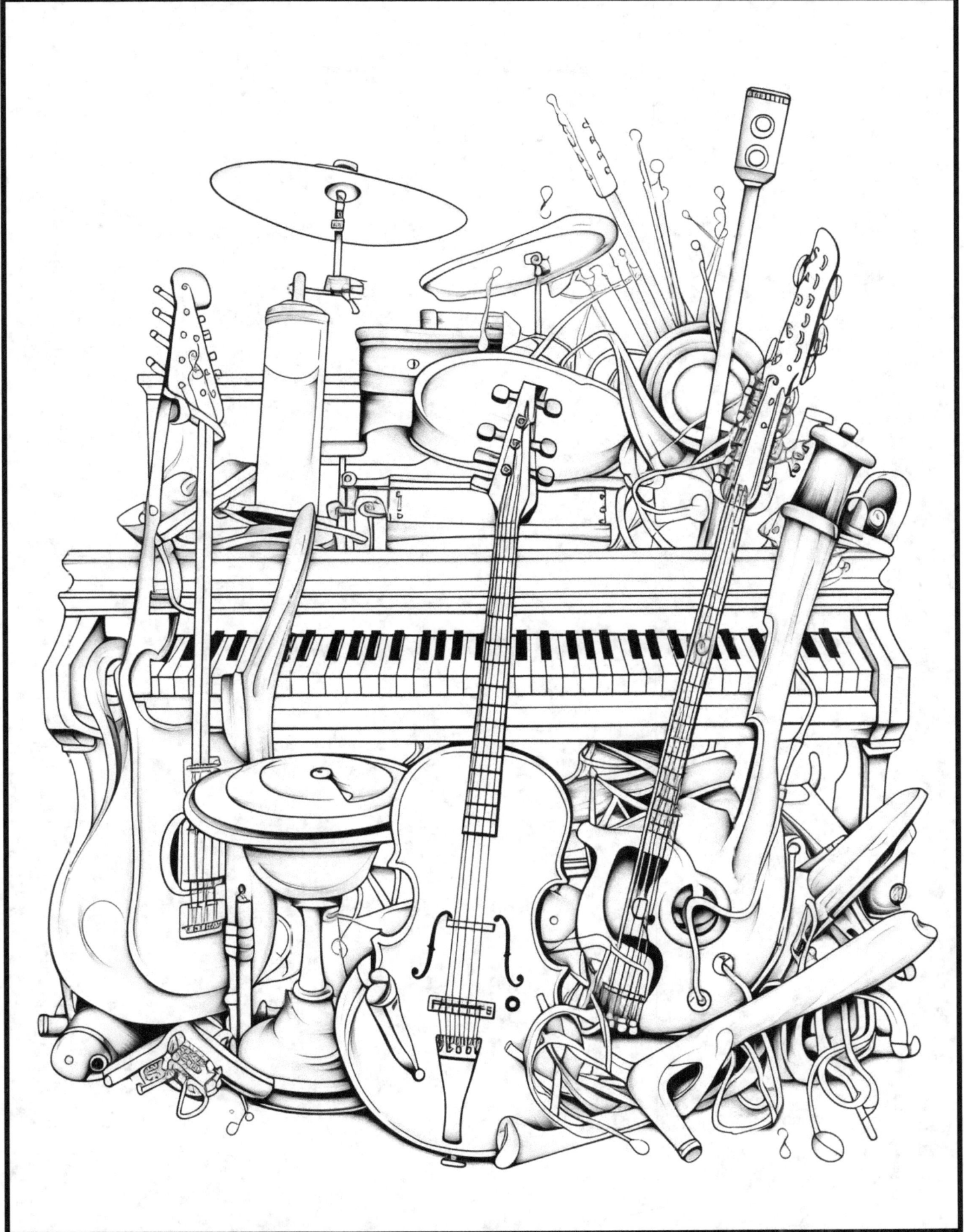

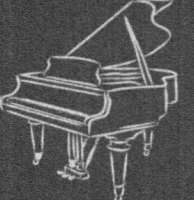

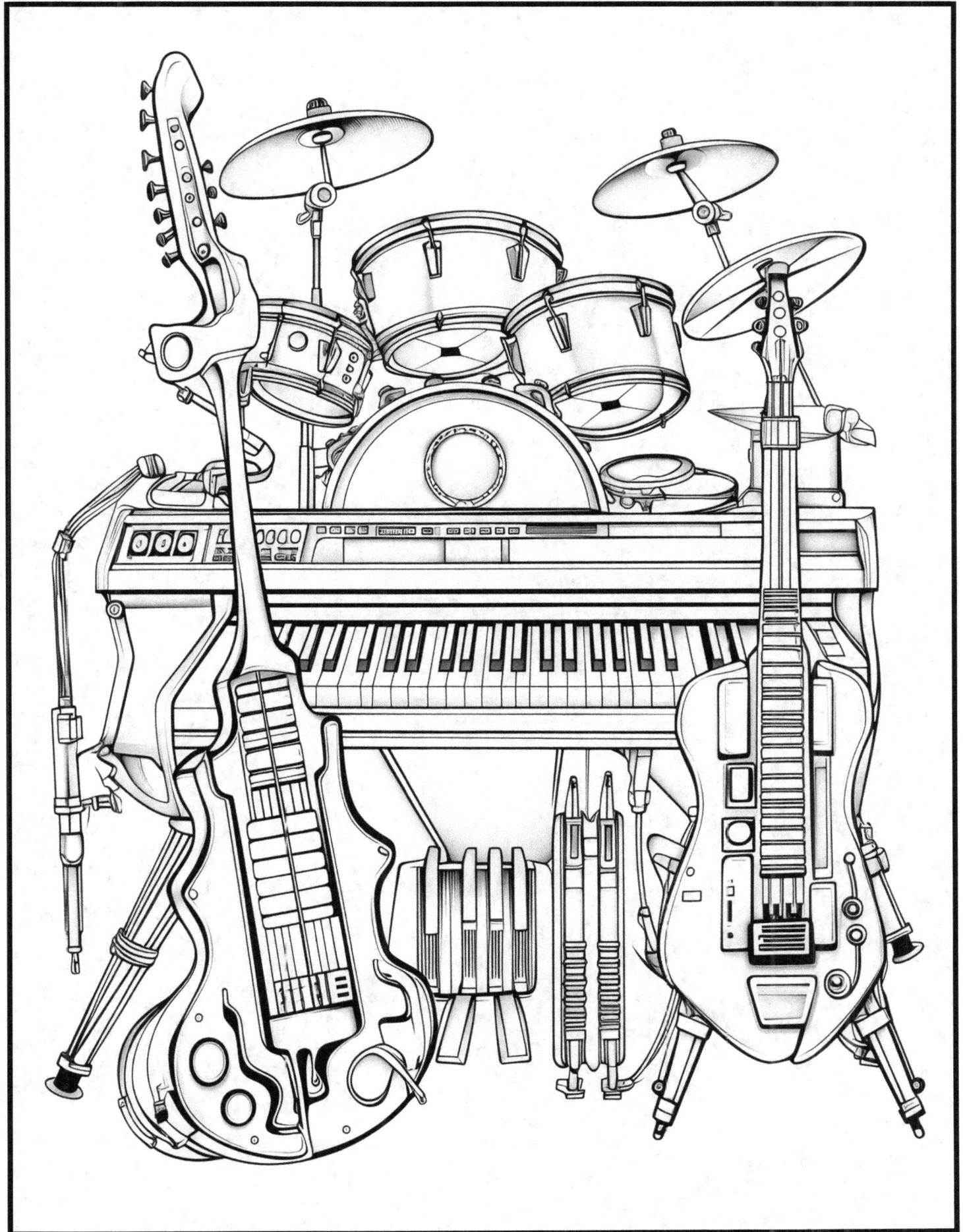

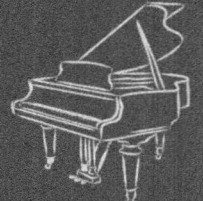

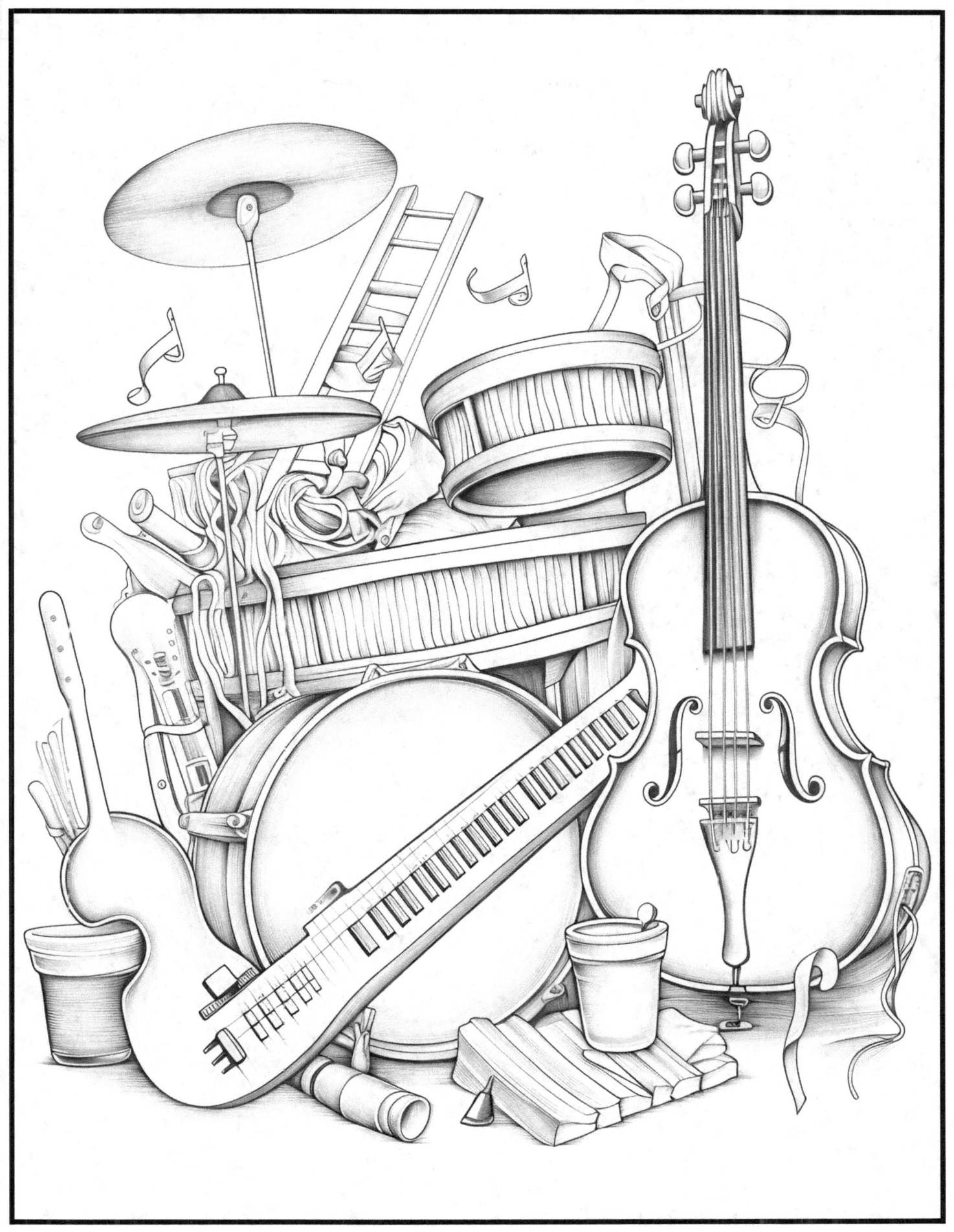

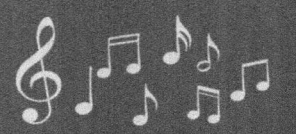
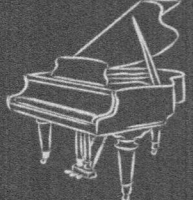

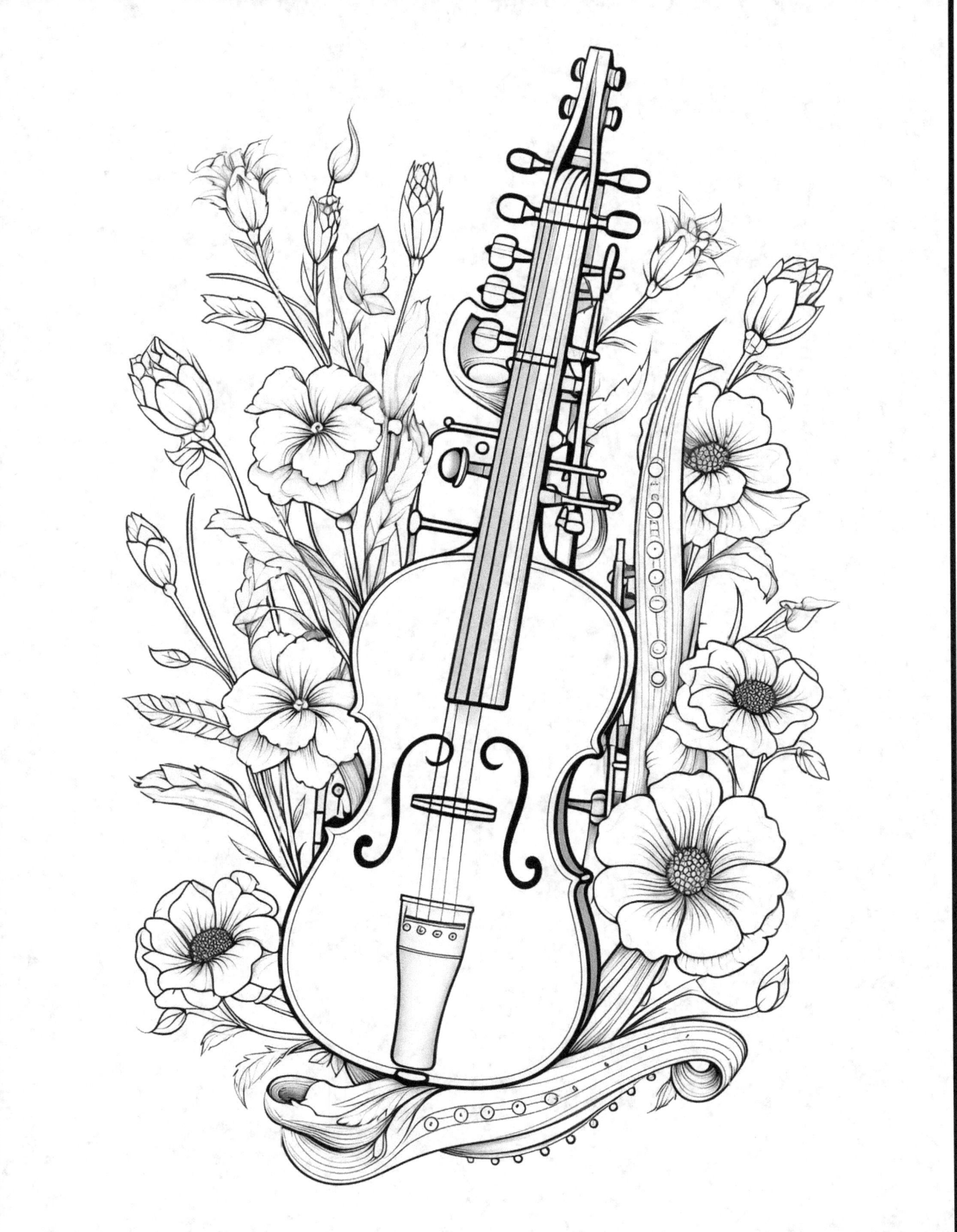

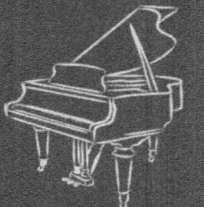

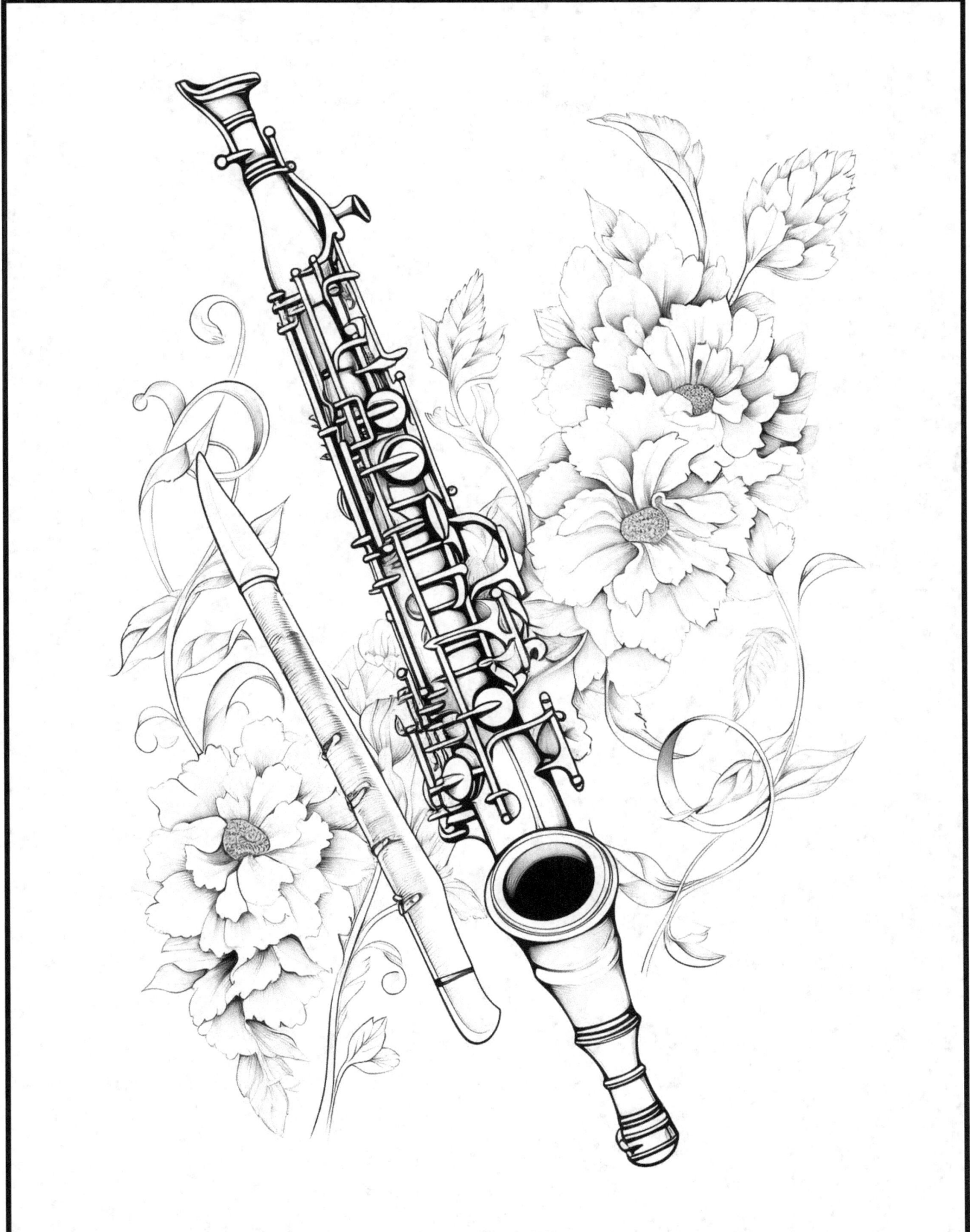

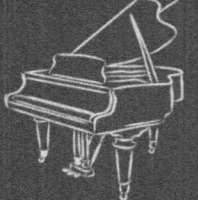

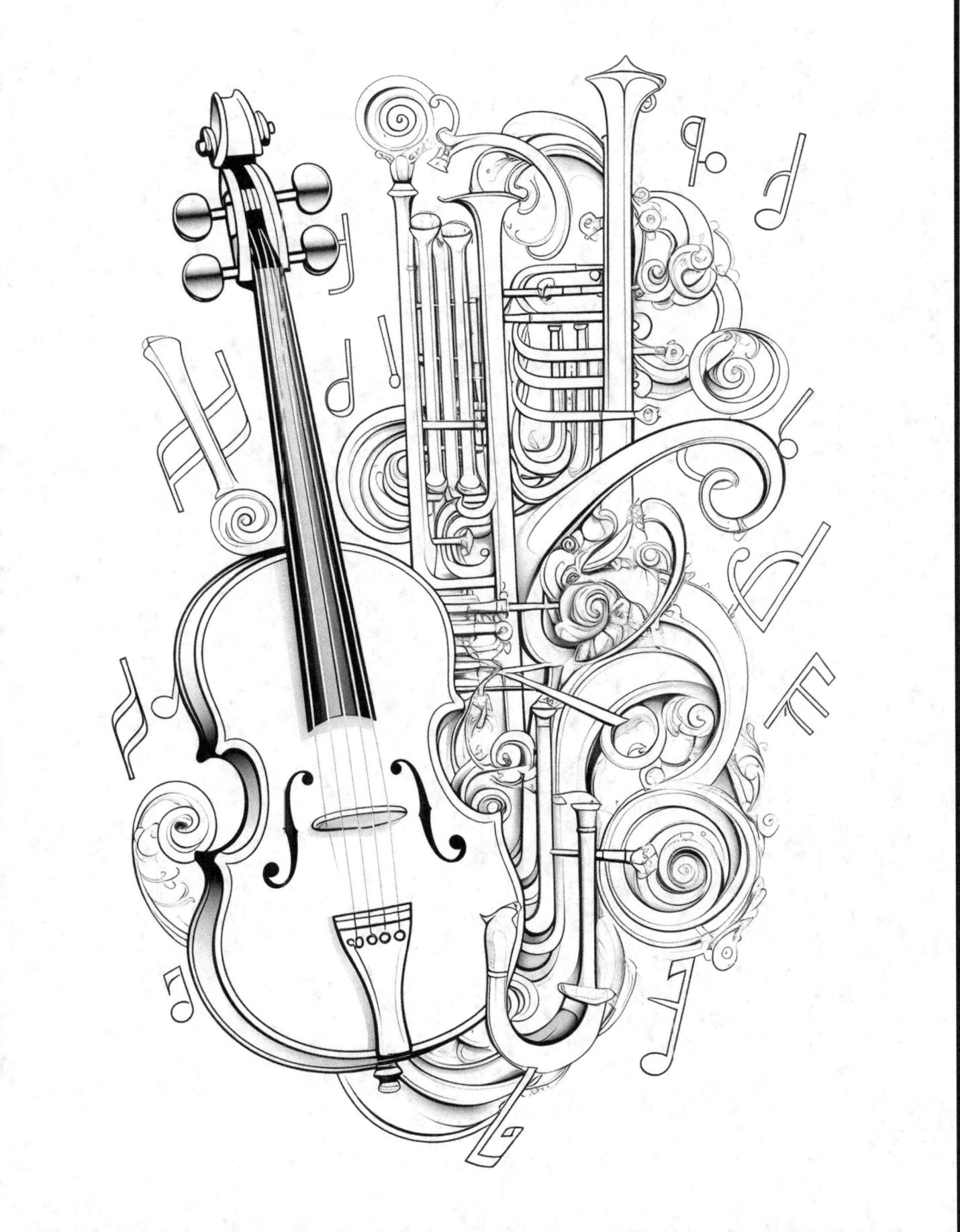

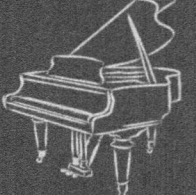

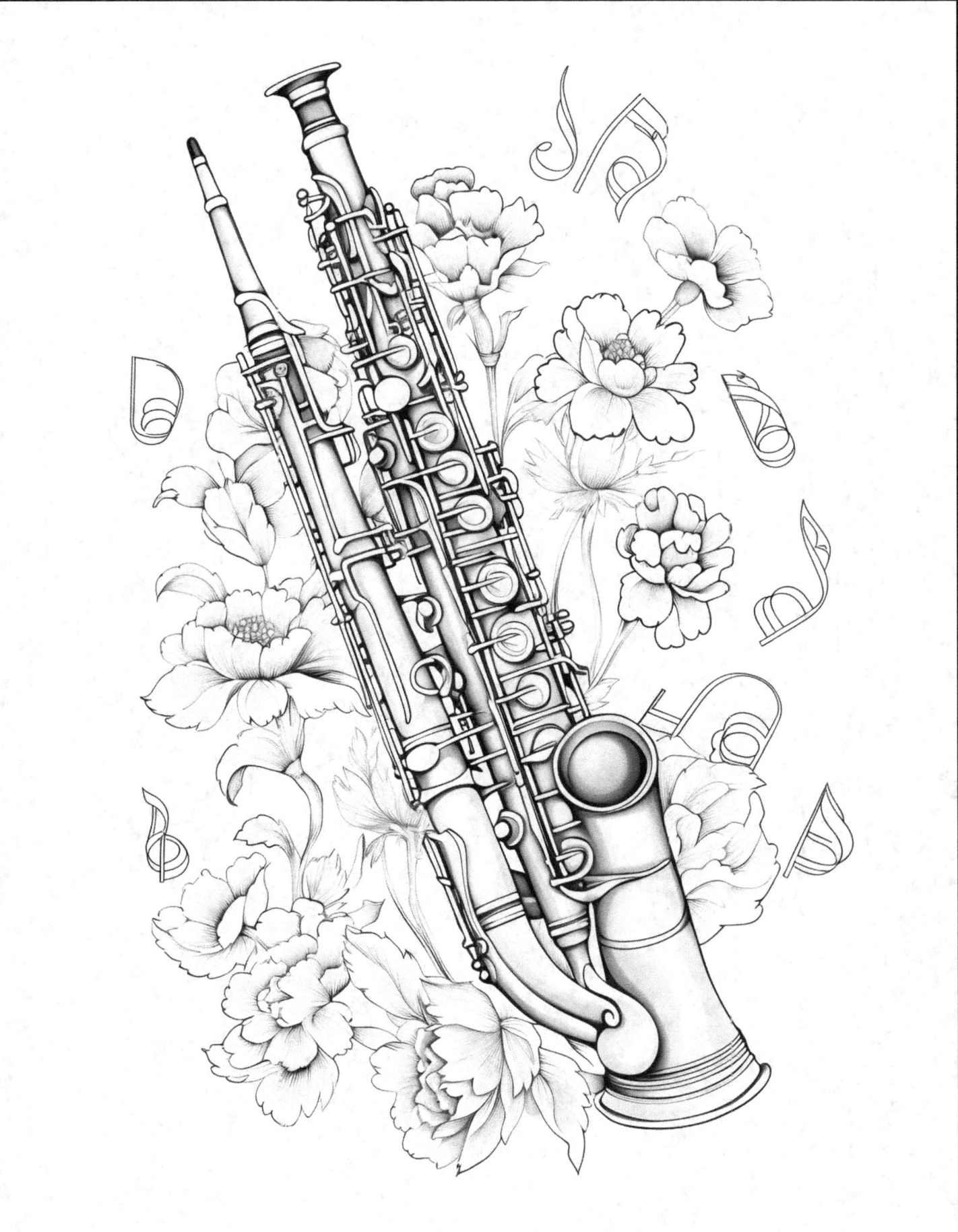

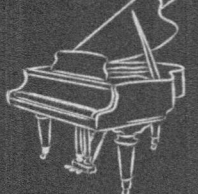

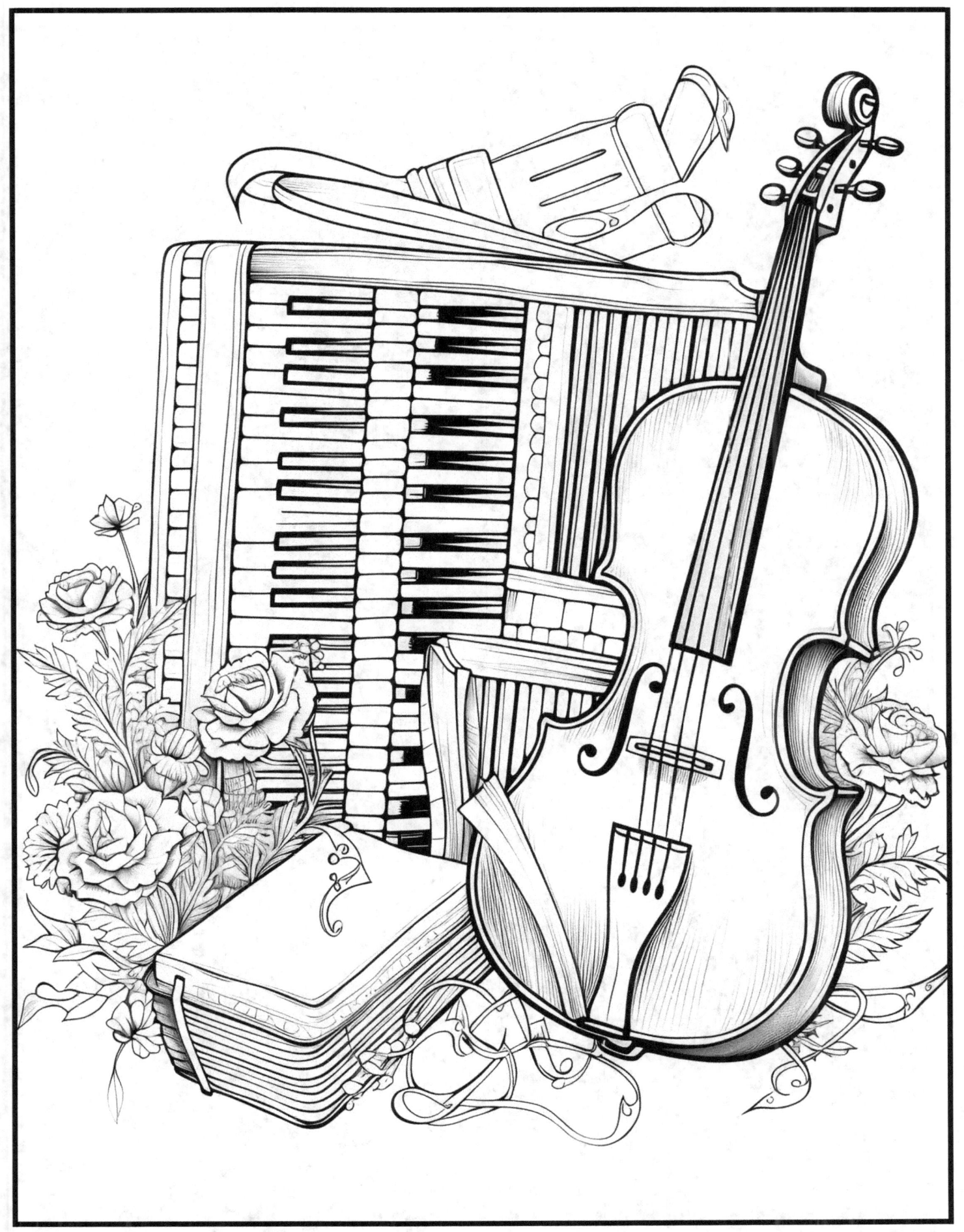

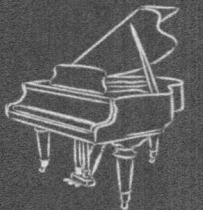

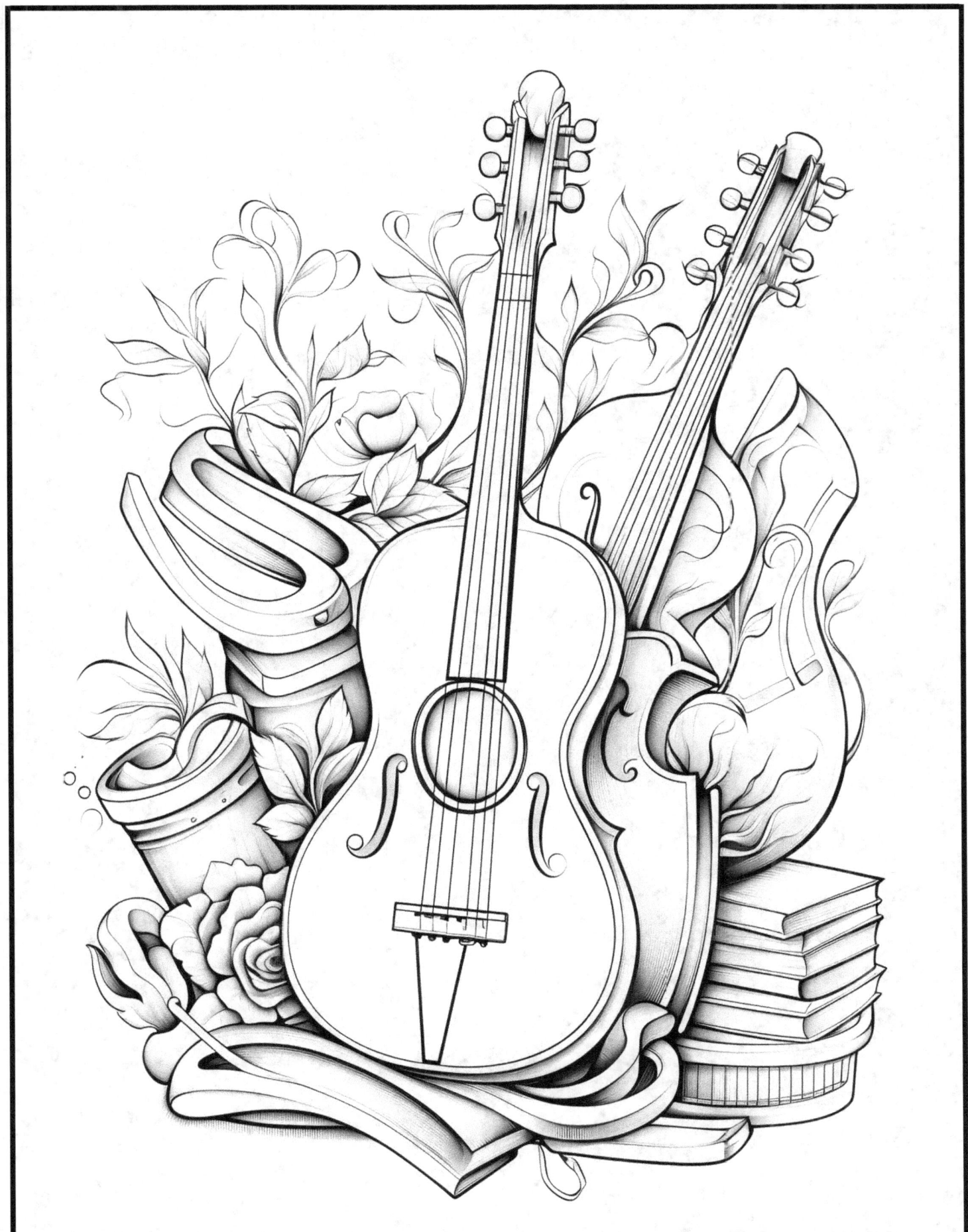

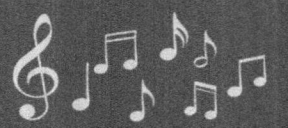
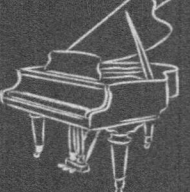

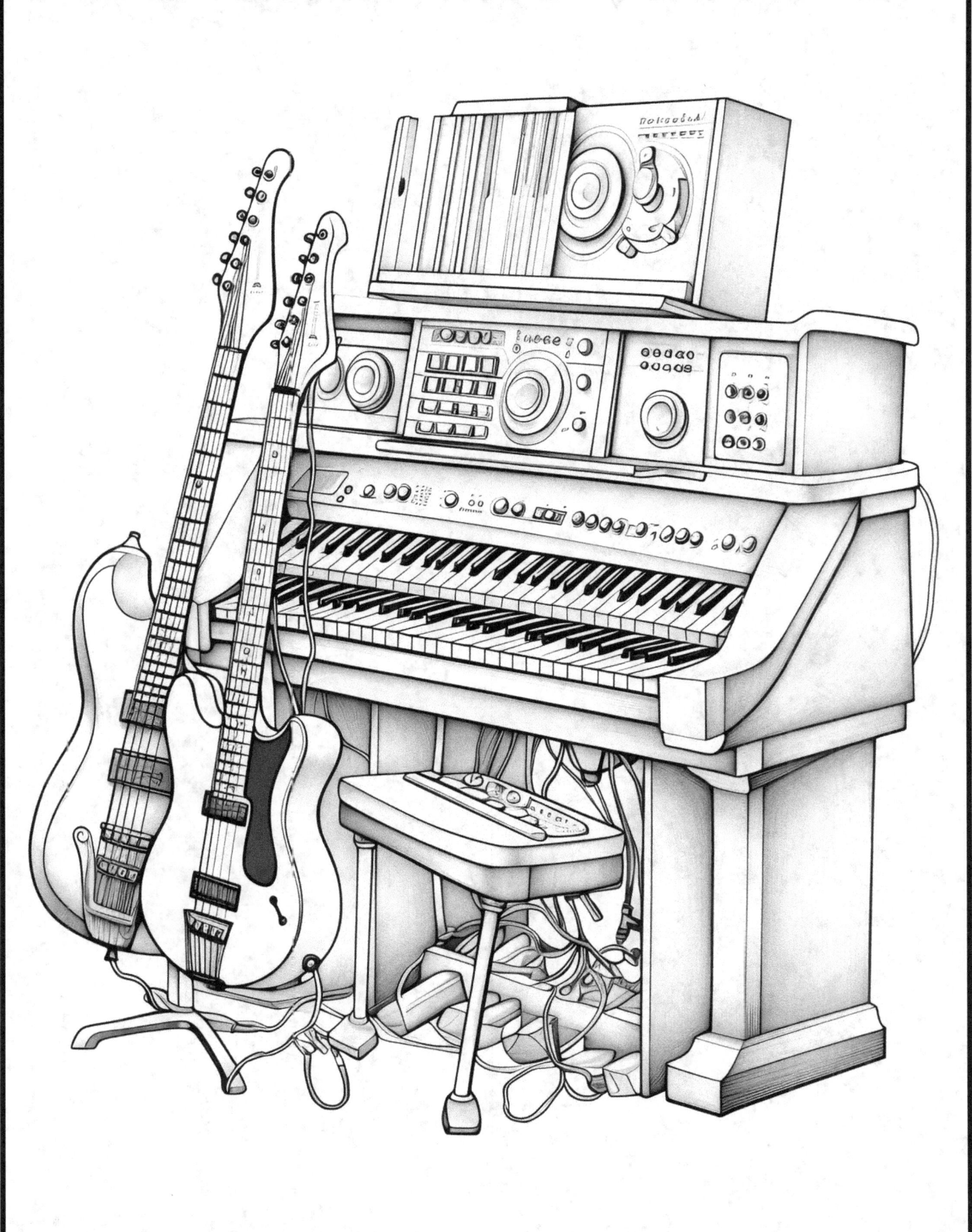

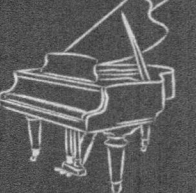

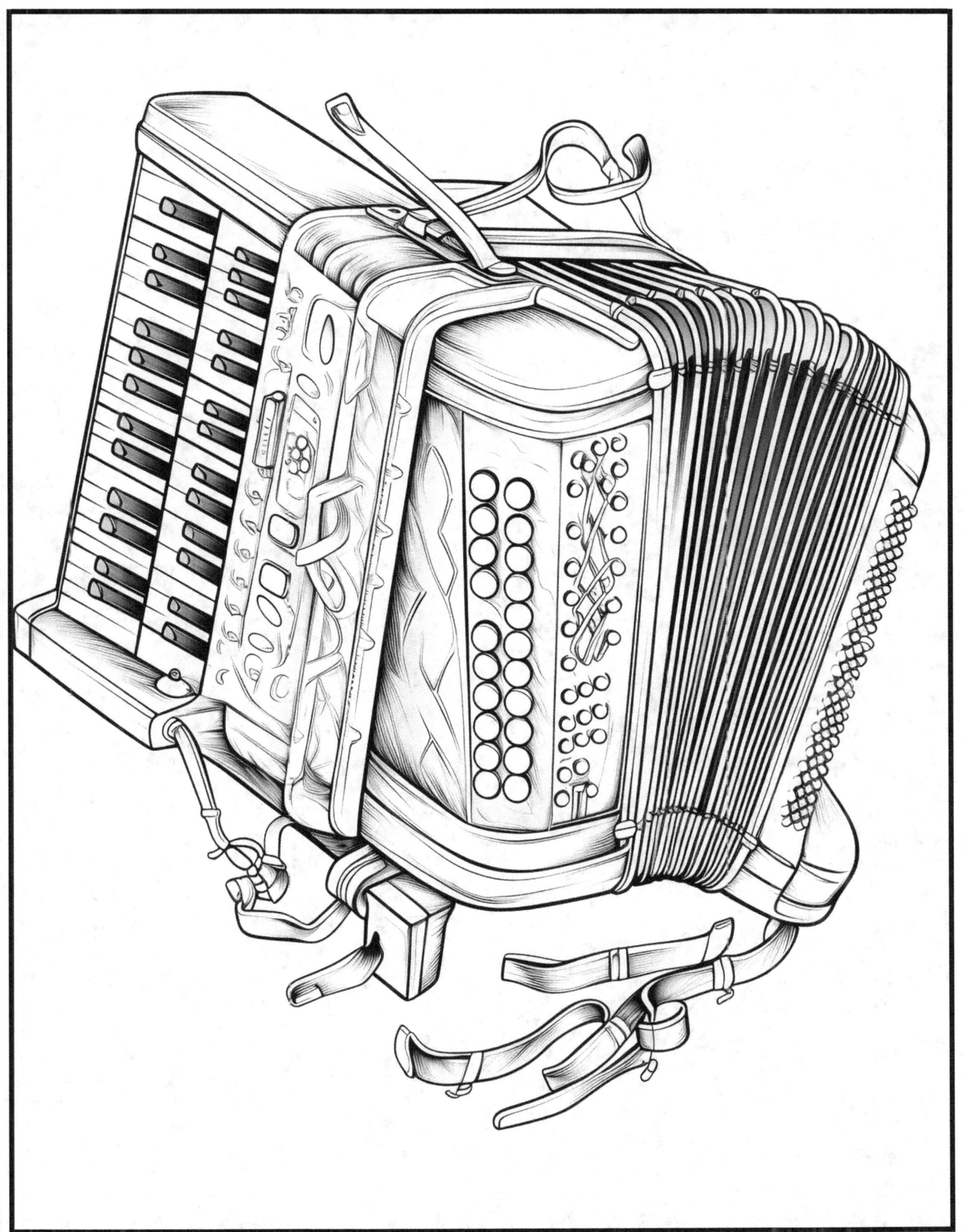

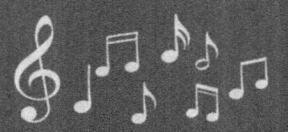
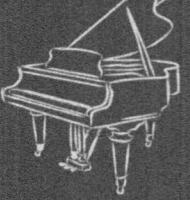

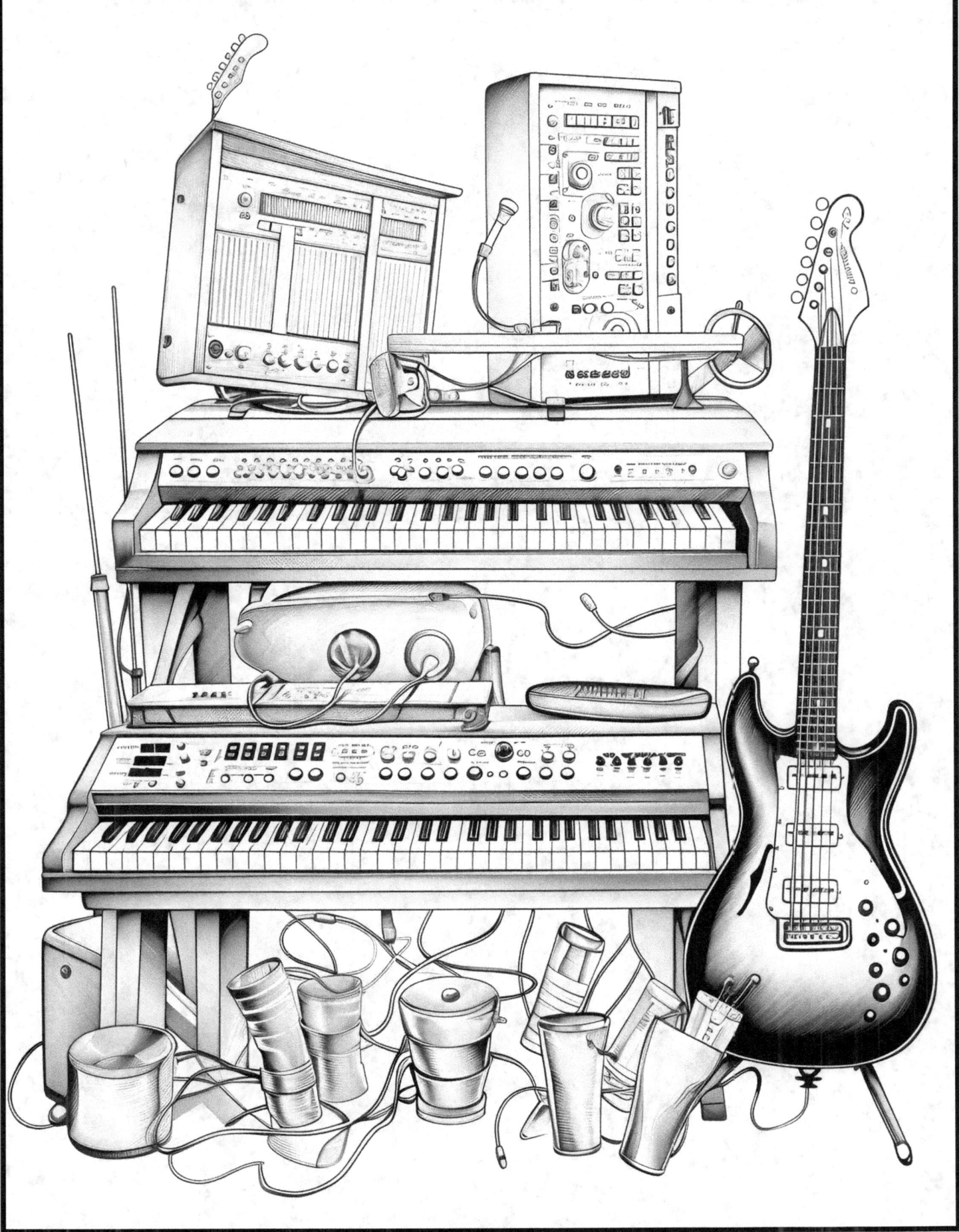

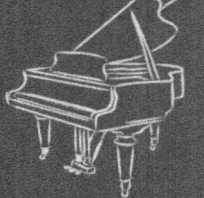

To all those who love music and art.

www.ingramcontent.com/pod-product-compliance
Lightning Source LLC
Chambersburg PA
CBHW082135290526
45794CB00008B/3050